KT-493-251

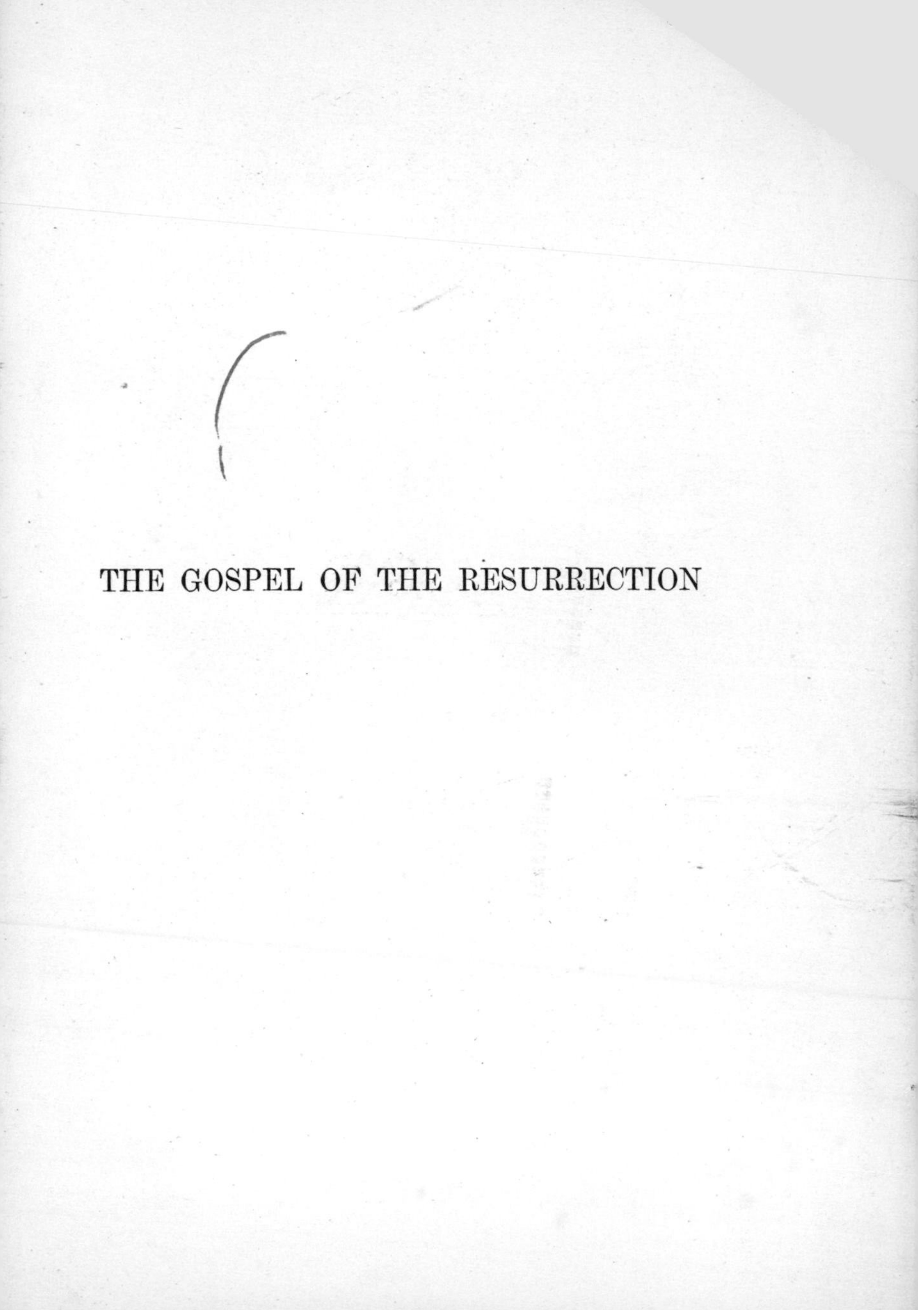

THE GOSPEL OF THE RESURRECTION

THE GOSPEL

OF

THE RESURRECTION

THOUGHTS ON ITS RELATION TO REASON AND HISTORY

BY

BROOKE FOSS WESTCOTT, D.D., D.C.L.

CANON OF WESTMINSTER
AND REGIUS PROFESSOR OF DIVINITY

London
MACMILLAN AND CO., LIMITED
NEW YORK: THE MACMILLAN COMPANY
1902

Εὐλόγως ὁ διδάσκαλος ἡμῶν ἔλεγεν,

ΓΙΝΕΣΘΕ ΤΡΑΠΕΖΙΤΑΙ ΔΟΚΙΜΟΙ

First Edition, 1866; *Second*, 1867; *Third*, 1874; *Fourth*, 1879; *Fifth*, 1884;
Sixth, 1887; *Seventh*, 1891; *Eighth*, 1898, 1902.

NOTICE TO THE FOURTH EDITION

In revising the following pages I have had the great advantage of considering two important criticisms upon its main argument, one by Mr. R. W. Macan in his Essay on *The Resurrection of Christ,* 1877, and the other by the Author of *Supernatural Religion,* in the third volume of his work, and in two papers in the *Fortnightly Review* for February and March 1878. It would be affectation to say that either writer has brought forward arguments which I had not considered previously to the best of my ability; but I gladly acknowledge the help which both have given me in understanding modes of thought which are foreign to my own. I hope that the few verbal changes and additions which I have made in the statement of my views may help to render my meaning clearer, where I find that it has been misapprehended. One or two errors have been corrected, and one or two difficulties have been touched upon more fully than before, where the reasoning of my critics or my own experience showed such changes to be necessary. But I have made the changes silently, for I cannot think that the pursuit of the highest Truth is a matter for personal controversy. No one, I feel, has a monopoly of Truth. It is enough that in defending the Truth which we know, we never consciously underrate or neglect the objections of opponents. The teacher who either presumes to claim the knowledge which he has not, or dissembles his own difficulties, carries in his own heart the elements of a stern and inevitable chastisement.

TRINITY COLLEGE, CAMBRIDGE,
13th May 1879.

NOTICE TO THE THIRD EDITION

BEFORE issuing a new edition of the present Essay I have carefully reconsidered the whole argument, and by the help of several kind critics have been enabled to correct (as I hope) some faults, and to remove some ambiguities, which had been overlooked before. I have not, however, made any attempt to alter the general character of the book. No one can feel more keenly than I do how often I must try the patience of my readers, but I believe that any one who has felt the difficulties which are touched upon, will be willing to follow out in detail the lines of thought which are suggested; and in subjects where all language necessarily falls short of the truth which we perceive "in many parts and in many fashions," it seems better to stir inquiry, if it may be, than to appear to anticipate and satisfy it.

Some recent speculations on the scope and foundation of Christianity show with singular clearness that even the most candid interpreters of the Gospel can still miss its scope. For it cannot, as far as I can see, be finally questioned by any student of the Apostolic records that the earliest known description of a Christian is "one who *believes on Christ*," and not "one who *believes Christ*." Or, in other words, a Christian is essentially one who throws himself with absolute trust upon a living Lord, and not simply one who endeavours to obey the commands and follow the example of a dead Teacher. The question at issue is not the observance of a certain number of definite precepts, but a view of the whole Universe, of all being and of all life, of man and of the world, and of GOD.

In this aspect the Resurrection is not an isolated fact, but emphatically a revelation (ch. ii. §§ 16 ff.). If the fragmentary accounts of the Resurrection were such as to yield a simple and consistent narrative of the restoration of the Lord to the circumstances of the earthly life which He lived before, it is not too much to say that the hope which they convey would be destroyed. The marvel of the records is that details which mark the identity of the Lord's person are combined naturally (so to speak) and in the same Gospel with details which mark the change in the conditions of His personal existence, as if those who put the facts together were conscious of no difficulty in the apparent contradiction from their actual realisation of the new

Truth. And when we come to combine their narratives we find it impossible to form any theory of the nature of the Resurrection as a fact like in kind to any other facts of our experience which is not at variance with some at least of the recorded details. Thus, if we take one series of events, the Resurrection might appear to have been a mere coming back to life: if we take another, it might appear to be a deduction from a series of apparitions. Either supposition would be more or less consistent with the ordinary course of things; but an examination of the records will not justify a simple choice between the two alternatives. In some cases again the manifestations carried with them instant conviction to those to whom they were made: in others they raised questionings and even left doubt. But so far from these variations creating a difficulty, they lead us to the fullest perception which as yet we are able to gain of the new life as a fact. If they are held firmly as a whole, they offer an adequate explanation of the faith of St. Paul. If, on the other hand, any one series of phenomena be disregarded, we lose something either of the reality or of the breadth of the revelation: there are features in the unquestionably contemporaneous faith of the Apostles which are left without an adequate explanation.[1]

[1] I have endeavoured to give a general view of the lessons of the different narratives in *The Revelation of the Risen Lord.*

Thus as we reflect upon the substance of the Apostolic records and the experience of the Church with more simplicity of heart and more complete self-devotion, the more nearly are we brought back to the words of St. Paul, *If thou shalt make the confession with thy mouth* JESUS *is* LORD, *and shalt believe in thy heart that God raised Him from the dead, thou shalt be saved.* The acknowledgment of the present sovereignty of *the Son of Man* in this earliest Creed (τὸ ῥῆμα) rests upon faith in the actual Resurrection of *the Son of Man;* and together these two facts—Christ's Sovereignty and Christ's Resurrection—offer to men the power and the motive which are required for a life of sacrifice and hope.

This elementary conception of Christianity as involving a living relation with One "who died and is alive again" may be of service in the prospect of immediate dangers. For it seems to be commonly admitted that once again we are approaching a great crisis in the history of human society and human thought; and many look with doubt, or even with more than doubt, on the adequacy of Christian Theology to meet and reconcile the conflicting elements which are rising around us. It is, indeed, confessed that our distinctive Faith—the Gospel of the Resurrection—contained within it the vital and constructive forces which were able to preserve the treasures of the old world from the shipwreck of the Roman Empire, to organise and guide the fresh energies of the northern nations, to receive and consecrate the recovered heritage of Greek art and Greek speculation; but there is still a vague fear that the dangers by which we are now menaced are greater than any which have gone before, greater than political dissolution, greater than triumphant barbarism, greater than paganised culture. It is perhaps necessary that it should be so. For while it is comparatively easy to estimate the relative value of forces from a distant and quiet vantage-ground, all that is seen through the dimness and mist of the struggle appears gigantic and alarming. Yet even at first sight we must acknowledge that the past victories of faith cannot but inspire us with confidence in entering on that struggle to which we are called, and at the same time furnish us with those lessons of experience which may free us from some natural fears. No one now questions that Christianity has been made richer and stronger by the loss of the imperial patronage with which it was once dignified, by the action of the restless freedom of the Teutonic spirit upon the personal apprehension of its teaching, by the calm light of ancient literature which reveals and harmonises a manifold variety in the providential dealings of GOD with man. And thus taught we can rejoice to believe that the coming *renaissance* of science will minister, no less than the past *renaissance* of culture has already done, to the abiding efficacy of the Truth which has been handed down to us.

But though we believe that it will be so, or rather because we believe that it will be so, it is well for us to prepare for the coming access of light, to take account of the whole scope of the Truth, to consider what belongs to its essence and what to the form in which it is embodied, to test the various modes by which men strive towards a fuller knowledge of it, to ascertain the relation which the particular fragment with which we happen for the time to be busied bears to the great sum to which it contributes. There is a constant and perilous tendency in partial study, and all study must be more or less partial, to exaggerate details or shapes of Truth, to pursue exclusively a method legitimate in one region, and so to apply it to inappropriate subjects, to neglect the ennobling inspiration which comes from a sense of the magnificence of the whole work in which we are allowed to take some small part. And this, which is true elsewhere, is most true of that study, which is of all the widest and grandest, the pursuit and setting forth of the science of Theology, to which all other sciences contribute, and in which they find their crown and consummation,—a unity of idea according to our present forms of thought, and the assurance of eternal worth.

In proportion, therefore, as the exposition of Christian Doctrine becomes more complicated, it becomes more necessary to strive to keep ever present to our minds the thought of Christ Himself, Incarnate, Crucified, Raised, Ascended, in whose Person and Work all doctrine is implicitly contained. And the study of the Bible and the study of the Church history are the chief means through which the Holy Spirit opens out the understanding of our personal faith. Through this double study pursued fearlessly and thoroughly, because it is pursued in the sight of God and in dependence on His Spirit, doctrine and ritual first become really intelligible: and though it is a dangerous thing to use the word "proof" of subjects to which no method of deduction or induction is applicable, this double study brings that conviction of the truth of Christianity on which the intellect as well as the soul of man can rest with absolute assurance. As we read the Holy Scriptures with more open minds, dissembling none of the difficulties by which they are beset, claiming for them no immunity from the ordinary processes of criticism, realising with the most strenuous endeavour every detail of their human characteristics, we shall learn what is meant by "living words," what is meant by "the inspiration of a book." As we follow the progress of the Christian society through conflicts and triumphs and disasters, through periods of threatening gloom and rekindled light, often checked and diverted but never stopped, often entangled and impeded by strange accretions but yet always able to cast them off, we shall feel that there is in it a power greater than that of man. Such inquiries, so far as they are undertaken in fellowship with Christ, will enable us to stand in a living relationship with prophets and apostles and confessors, so that their words will come to us not as a tradition or a formula, but as fresh utterances called out by the actual needs of men like ourselves, from the hearts of those who sympathised with them. We shall find that we are the inheritors of a life and not of a system, of a life which is a pledge of the unity of all that is seen and temporal with that which is unseen and eternal.

While, therefore, I do not desire to dissemble or to exaggerate the gravity and even the strangeness of the new trial of Faith, the occasion is, as I believe, more full of hope than of fear. I cannot doubt what the Church of England may do, within whose reach are placed the three great springs of power which have been given separately to other Churches, the simplicity of a pure creed, the strength of a continuous organisation, the freedom of personal faith. I cannot doubt what our own University may do, in which a grave and sober intellectual discipline prepares men for patient criticism and large-minded research. But still the time of labour is short, and if we waste it there appears to be no further prospect that the work to which we are called will be hereafter accomplished.

But it cannot be needful to dwell on the possibility of this most disastrous failure. The symptoms of dissension and confusion and doubt among us are rather indications of the restless unsatisfied energy of newly awakened life than warnings of decay and dissolution. We are, indeed, forced to confess that we have not yet shown practically what Theology is, what the Church is, what doctrine is. We have allowed questions of social and national right to be discussed without reference to that infinite Truth which, though above our grasp, is yet a light by which we can guide our course. We have stood as Christians so far aloof from secular speculation that we have almost forgotten that it must be through these lower studies that our apprehension of our own unchanging message is advanced. We have so persistently dissembled the power of the Gospel—the historical reconciliation of GOD with the world and man—that it is pardonable if those who judge of it by us should doubt whether it is anything more efficacious and inspiring than the pathetic guesses which adorn the writings of philosophy. But while we deplore our faithlessness we can rise out of it. And this we must do, if once again we see Christ as the ascended Lord, and let the light of His glorious Person fall upon our life and upon all life.

B. F. W.

TRINITY COLLEGE,
23d February 1874.

NOTICE TO THE SECOND EDITION

By the kindness of many old and some new friends I have been enabled to correct and modify and supplement many of the details in my original Essay; but a careful and (as I trust) impartial review suggests to me no change in the main argument. Indeed every symptom of the theological controversies of our own day points most distinctly to the paramount necessity of a historical appreciation of the origin and development of the Church as the key to the wider questions which are opening before us. The Epistle to the Ephesians and the writings of St. John contain in a divine commentary on the Resurrection, of which Christian history is the gradual and partial fulfilment, the complete solution of the greatest problems to which the thoughts of men are now being turned, the Solidarity of Humanity and the relation of our World to the whole Kosmos.

If my leisure and health had allowed me, I should have added a final chapter on the *Resurrection and the*

World, which has for some time been drawn up in outline. In this it would have been necessary to take account of the "Positive Religion" of M. Comte, which in many of its characteristic dogmas appears to cast unexpected light upon neglected Christian Truths. The system offers in fact a very noble, though a very partial view of Christianity in its political and social aspects, but without the one essential foundation of a historic CHRIST.[1]

It may perhaps be worth while to state that the sketch of the Essay was made many years ago, and that it was written in 1864 and printed in the early part of 1865, though it was not published till 1866. I cannot therefore take to myself the credit which a friendly critic gave me of "popularising" arguments on miracles which were in time subsequent to my own and wholly independent of them. The coincidence of reasoning, if it exists, as I take for granted, is most satisfactory, though practically I believe that there can be little difference of opinion on this subject between those who will take the trouble to think it out in all its cardinal bearings.

But all speculation leaves the profound conviction that life is stronger than thought; and the present season itself proclaims more eloquently than many words the

[1] [I have now added as an appendix an Essay which marks what appear to me to be the chief points for consideration under this head. 1874.]

Gospel of the Resurrection, and, if we are faithful, more convincingly. If each Christian would openly "confess with his mouth" the truth which he "believes in his heart," the world would gladly yield to the glorious greeting of our Easter morning, "Christ is risen."

B. F. W.

St. Leonard's,
Easter Eve, 1867.

PREFACE

'Εὰν ὁμολογήσῃς τὸ ῥῆμα ἐν τῷ στόματί σου ὅτι Κύριος 'Ιησοῦς καὶ πιστεύσῃς ἐν τῇ καρδίᾳ σου ὅτι ὁ θεὸς αὐτὸν ἤγειρεν ἐκ νεκρῶν, σωθήσῃ.

THE present Essay is an endeavour to consider some of the elementary truths of Christianity as a miraculous Revelation from the side of History and Reason. There seems to be a growing impression, for it is too vague to be called a belief, that such a fact as the Resurrection cannot be brought into harmony with what we see of the life of the world or what we feel of the laws of individual thought. The opponents of Christianity tacitly assume that a miracle must be explained away; and its defenders neglect to notice the manifold lines of culture and thought which converge towards the central lessons of the Gospel and again start from them with the promise of richer fruitfulness. If the arguments which are here adduced are valid they will go far to prove that the Resurrection, with all that it includes, is the key to the history of man, and the complement of reason. At least they will show that the supposed incompatibility of a devout belief in the Life of Christ with a broad view of the course of human progress and a frank trust in the laws of our own minds, is wholly imaginary. Indeed it is not too much to assert that the fact of the Resurrection (as the typical miracle of the Gospel) becomes more natural as we take a more comprehensive view of history, and more harmonious with reason as we interrogate our instincts more closely. A conviction of the certainty of the facts of the Gospel seems to be best gained either by the most general or by the most personal view of their import. They fill up the most critical place in the great record of the progress of mankind; and they satisfy wants which each man feels for himself. Christianity has many sides; and those are by no means the least noble which are thus opened to the student of life and thought.

The object which I proposed to myself necessarily involved a mode of treatment wholly untheological. Many topics consequently are dealt with otherwise than they would be dealt with in a doctrinal exposition; and many are wholly omitted which would have found a place in such a work. But while I have endeavoured to avoid technical language, I trust that no word in the Essay will be found at variance with the fulness of Catholic truth.

He who has long pondered over a train of reasoning becomes unable to detect its weak points. It is so, I am conscious, with what I now offer to the criticism of others. But the only desire which he can have who writes on such a subject must be to learn the truth fully that in turn he may speak it. The questions which are raised are momentous and personal. If we believe that the answers which I have given are true or like the truth, our modes of thought and our lives must bear witness to our Faith.

And it seems impossible not to acknowledge that the recognition of the Resurrection as a fact which has moulded the thoughts of Christians and yet retains the fulness of its vital power, is less spontáneous and instinctive among us than it ought to be in a Christian age. Nay, more, its teachings are not so much neglected as absolutely unperceived in popular estimates of what Christianity claims to be and is. Two passages from recent works, which have perhaps nothing else in common, will illustrate my meaning. "There is no hope," we are told, "of a good understanding with Orientals [*i.e.* Muslims] until Western Christians can bring themselves to recognise what there is of common faith contained in the two religions; *the real difference consists in all the class of notions and feelings* (very important ones, no doubt) *which we derive not from the Gospels but from Greece and Rome,* and which are altogether wanting here [in the East]." And again: "Christian morality (so called) has all the characters of a reaction ; it is, in great part, a protest against Paganism, *Its ideal is negative rather than positive: passive rather than active: Innocence rather than Nobleness: Abstinence from Evil rather than energetic Pursuit of Good;* in its precepts (as has been well said) 'thou shalt not' predominates unduly over 'thou shalt.' . . . It holds out the hope of heaven and the threat of hell as the appointed and appropriate motives to a virtuous life. . . . Even in the morality of private life, *whatever exists of magnanimity, high-mindedness, personal dignity, even the sense of honour, is derived from the purely human, not the religious part of our education, and never could have grown out of a standard of ethics in which the only worth, professedly recognised, is that of obedience."* Now, apart from all other criticism, to which these statements lie open, it is not too much to say that they absolutely could not have been written if their authors had realised that Christianity is emphatically the Gospel of the Resurrection, in which fact lies a spring of human dignity and social fellowship infinitely deeper and fuller than anything which was anticipated in classical teaching.

During the passage of the Essay through the press I have been indebted to many friends, and especially to one, for important suggestions and criticisms. Of some I have been able to make use: others, if an opportunity be given me, I shall hope to use hereafter; for all I render them my sincere thanks. And the deepest obligation which any reader can confer upon me will be to point out whatever seems obscure or faulty or erroneous in what is here advanced. For writer and for reader Truth is the common aim. The subject *is not a vain thing for us: it is our life.*

B. F. W.

CAMBRIDGE,
16*th December* 1865.

CONTENTS[1]

INTRODUCTION

[1] The numbering of the sections is made continuous, but the new sections are marked by an asterisk. [Ed. 2.]

CHAPTER I

CHAPTER II

CHAPTER III

STATEMENT OF THE QUESTION

Καλὸν τὸ ἆθλον καὶ ἡ ἐλπὶς μεγάλη.—Plato.

1. Jean Paul, in one of his magnificent Dreams, has endeavoured to present to the mind an image of the infinite extent and fulness of the Universe. He represents his own disembodied Spirit as carried by thought from system to system through the starry skies under the conduct of some Angel of light. Wearied at length, and bowed down with the overwhelming sense of his littleness as he traverses the desolate intervals between world and world, he prays that he may go no farther: "I am lonely in creation; lonelier in these wastes. The full world is great; but Vacancy is greater." And the answer came "In the sight of God there is no Vacancy. Even now, O child of man, let thy quickened eye behold, and thy dreaming heart embrace the depths of Being which are around thee." Then his eye was opened and a sea of light filled all the spaces which had seemed desolate before, and his heart felt the presence of an unspeakable power, swelling in varied forms of existence around him. Suns and planets were seen to float as mere specks in the vast ocean of life which was revealed to him. For a time he was conscious of no pain.

Immeasurable joy and thanksgiving filled his soul. But in this glorious splendour his guide had vanished. He was alone in the midst of life, and he yearned for some companionship. "Then there came sailing onwards," he continues, "from the depth, through the galaxies of stars, a dark globe along the sea of light; and a human form, as a child, stood upon it, which neither changed nor yet grew greater as it drew near. At last I recognised our Earth before me, and on it the Child JESUS. and He looked upon me with a look so bright and gentle and loving, that I awoke for love and joy."

2. The thought which inspires this grand vision is that which I now wish to develop and confirm. It is my object to show that a belief in the Resurrection of our Lord is not indeed the solution (for that we cannot gain), but the illumination of the mysteries of life: that in this fact the apparent contradictions of the immensity and insignificance of the individual are harmonised that in this lies an end to which pre-Christian history converged, a spring from which post-Christian history flows: that in this man finds the only perfect consecration of his entire nature: that in this there is contained a promise for the future which removes, as far as may be, the sense of isolation which belongs to our finite nature, and unites our world again to the absolute and eternal: that in this, to sum up all briefly, we may contemplate Christianity in relation to history, to man, and to the future, not as a vague idea, or as a set of dogmas, or even as a system, but as the witness to actual

events, in the substantial reality of which lies all its power and all its hope.

3. At the outset it is important to define the field within which the foundation of our inquiry lies, and to close it within the narrowest limits. It includes only the Cross and the Sepulchre. It is open to the full light of day. The Death, the Burial, and the Resurrection of Christ claim to be facts exactly in the same sense, to be supported by evidence essentially identical in kind, and to be bound together indissolubly as the groundwork of the Christian Faith. If they are true, then they will be seen to form the centre round which other truths group themselves, not less real, nor less significant, though they are not equally capable of being directly subjected to historical tests. If they are not true, then "is our faith vain." Christianity is a name and nothing more, a sentiment, an aspiration, the expression and not the satisfaction of human need.

4. The natural indistinctness of common language leaves room for a vague impression that in this case there is some mean between truth and falsehood: that though the Resurrection was not a fact (as the Crucifixion was a fact), yet it was something more than a fiction: that it expressed (it may be) an intuition or a divine belief. Yet it is obvious that the power of the Resurrection, as the ground of religious hope, lies in the very circumstance that the event which changed the whole character of the disciples was external to them,

independent of them, unexpected by them. We are speaking here, of course, of things as they present themselves to the senses, and in this light the Resurrection claims to have been so far a fact of the same order as the Burial of the Lord. Its objectivity is essential to its significance. A conviction that a particular person had risen again, when he had *not*, is simply false, however it may have been produced. And if the conviction embodies itself in a circumstantial narrative of facts intended to establish the imaginary event, the narrative is simply a falsehood and nothing more. There are cases, as, for example, in the description of the tumult of a battle, where fictitious or unreal details convey a relatively true idea of the whole. It is obviously impossible either to record or to apprehend the multitudinous phases of action which go to fill up a complicated and changing scene; and the genius of an artist may be able to convey to others the reality which he has himself grasped through representative incidents moulded to his purpose. It might be so, within certain limits, with the details of the Resurrection. But "if Christ be not risen," it is the whole and not the details which, on such a supposition, is imaginary. The Resurrection then is either a fact in itself wholly independent of those who were witnesses to it, or it is a fiction—it matters not whether designed or undesigned—on which no belief can be founded. It is a real link between the seen and the unseen worlds, or it is at best the expression of a human instinct. Christ has escaped from the corruption of death; or men, as far as the future is concerned, are exactly where they were before He came. Whatever may be the civilising power of Christian morality, it can throw no light upon the grave. If the Resurrection be not true in the same sense in which the Passion is true, then Death still remains the great conqueror. As far as all experience goes, no pledge has been given to us of his defeat. A splendid guess, an inextinguishable desire, alone have sought to pierce the darkness beyond the tomb, if JESUS has not (as we believe) borne our human nature into the presence of GOD.

5. When once we grasp clearly the momentous interests which are involved in the belief in the Resurrection, we shall be prepared to understand how it formed the central point of the Apostolic teaching; and yet more than this, how the event itself is the central point of history, primarily of religious history, and then of civil history of which that is the soul. It often seems indeed as if we do not realise the vastness of the consequences which it brings. An influential Christian teacher has said that the Resurrection belongs to the teaching on Scripture rather than to the teaching on the Person of Christ, forgetting that faith in Christ as the Saviour, so far as this was a Gospel for the world, did not precede but follow it. Even those who hold most firmly to a faith in the Resurrection are tempted to regard it as a doctrine rather than as a fact, as an article of belief rather than as a sensible ground of hope. Gradually we have been led to dissociate faith in the resurrection

of the body from the actual Resurrection of Christ, which is the earnest of it. And not unfrequently we substitute for the fulness of the Christian creed the purely philosophic conception of an immortality of the soul, which surrenders, as we shall see hereafter, the idea of the continuance of our complete personal existence. But according to the divine instinct of the first age, the message of the Resurrection sums up in one fact the teaching of the Gospel. It is the one central link between the seen and the unseen. We cannot allow our thoughts to be vague or undecided upon it with impunity. We must place it in the very front of our confession, with all that it includes, or we must be prepared to lay aside the Christian name. Even in its ethical aspect Christianity does not offer a system of morality, but a universal principle of morality which springs out of the Resurrection. The elements of dogma and morality are indeed inseparably united in the Resurrection of Christ; for the same fact which reveals the glory of the Lord, reveals at the same time the destiny of man and the permanence of all that goes to make up the fulness of human life. If the Resurrection be not true, the basis of Christian morality, no less than the basis of Christian theology, is gone. The issue cannot be stated too broadly. We are not Christians unless we are clear in our confession on this point. To preach the fact of Resurrection was the first function of the Evangelists; to embody the doctrine of the Resurrection is the great office of the Church; to learn the meaning of the Resurrection is the task not of one age only, but of all. Yet there seem to be times when the truth has a special significance: times, like our own, when the spirit of material progress tends to confine the thoughts of men within the limits of its own domain; when we are in constant danger of forgetting the larger relationships of human existence, because we find within us and around us enough to distract and occupy our thoughts; when the sense of the infinite vastness (so to speak) of our present finite being turns the soul away from its natural aspirations towards the absolute and the unseen.

6. This is one aspect of our subject. The Resurrection is a revelation, so far as such a revelation is possible, of the spiritual world and of our own connection with it. But it has also another aspect as a fact in the common history of the world. Its essentially objective character is not less important than its divine message. For we may notice that a religion which is to move the world must be based on a history. A religion drawn solely from the individual consciousness of man can only reflect a particular form of intellectual development. Its influence is limited by the mould in which it is cast. Its applicability is confined to those who have attained to a special culture. Even to the last it is essentially of the mind and not of the heart or of the life. This is obvious equally from the record of the speculations on Natural Theology, and from the history of all those religions which have had any power in the world. A subjective religion brings with it no element

of progress and cannot lift man out of himself. A historical revelation alone can present GOD as an object of personal love. The external world answering to human instinct suggests the conception of His eternal power, but offers nothing which justifies in us the confidence of "sons." Man is but one of the many elements of creation, and cannot arrogate to himself any special relationship with his Maker. Pure Theism is unable to form a living religion. Mahommedanism lost all religious power in a few generations. Judaism survived for fifteen centuries every form of assault in virtue of the records of a past deliverance on which it was based, and the hope of a future Deliverer which it included.

7. Briefly, the Gospel of the Resurrection harmonises in itself the objective and subjective elements of religion. On the one hand it reposes on a fact which, however unique, yet claims to belong to the circle of human experience. On the other hand the fact is such that its personal appropriation offers the widest scope for the energies of spiritual life. The Resurrection is sufficiently definite to take religion out of the domain of caprice and rest its hopes upon a foundation external to the believer; and it is so far-reaching in its ultimate significance as to present itself to every age and every soul with a fresh power. It gives faith a firm standing ground in history, and at the same time opens a boundless vision of the future development of our present powers. It brings down dogma to earth, and then vindicates the infinitude of the issues of temporal

existence. By the definiteness of its actual occurrence it gives dignity to all human action: by the universality of its import it lifts the thoughts of the believer from the man to the race and to the world. It stands, so to speak, midway between the seen and the unseen: it belongs equally to the spiritual and to the material order, and it reconciles both: it gives immediate reality to the one by the manifestation of the Son of man, who "came forth from the Father and went to the Father"; it ennobles the other by the revelation of a divine presence in the world according to His word, Who said, "Lo, I am with you all the days." In both respects its teaching is essential to Christianity. Exactly in proportion as it is lost sight of in the popular Creed, doctrine is divorced from life, and the broad promises of divine hope are lost in an individual struggle after good.

8. It is possible that individual exceptions may be found to the truth of these statements. Faith is indeed without question the spring of all progressive or universal religion; and the essence of faith lies in the transference of trust to something outside the believer. Yet, on the other hand, some great souls appear to have an immediate perception of isolated truths, so that in their case a thought becomes a distinct reality, contemplated, as it were, apart from the thinker. For such men faith in a thought is possible, and is the source of all that approaches most nearly to a new creation in human history. These solitary heroes can in some measure at

least live as seeing the unseen by the force of their innate power; but for the mass faith needs some outward pledge to rest upon, and some outward fact to call it into action. Exactly in proportion as the popular idea of religion is separated from the personal relation of the worshipper to the Deity, attested (or supposed to be attested) by historical manifestations, the worship itself degenerates into a discipline or a form. Even Christianity is capable of such a degradation; but we need only to go back to the Evangelists to regain a pure conception of its majesty. As it is seen in their narratives it satisfies equally the wants of the few and of the many; and that most signally in the message of the Resurrection, which was the assurance of the establishment of the kingdom of GOD. The facts of the visible Life of Christ are for all time a living Gospel; and the doctrine which they include meets and carries forward the boldest speculations of philosophy.

9. For it is evident that the events recorded by the Evangelists, while they are most truly historical, are not merely history. Their significance is not in the past only or even chiefly. And so also the evidence by which they are supported is not simply that of direct testimony. The authority of testimony is supplemented by that of the instinct[1] within us which recognises that the idea of a Divine Revelation corresponds with the essential

[1] The word is open to many objections, but I can find no other to express the spiritual impulse through which man's constitution expresses itself, as it is slowly trained by the circumstances of life. Experience shows that it is as much a part of his nature to turn to

wants of man. Man feels that he was born for God, and looks for some sign to assure him of the reality of a fellowship with the unseen. The feeling will show itself in the course of the whole education of humanity in many ways, but it is not without its appropriate discipline. A Divine Revelation must from the very nature of the case tend to satisfy the loftiest conception which can be formed of man's destiny. If it does not do so, it is condemned by the instinct which looks for it. Thus in discussing the truth of the Resurrection as a fact it is impossible not to take into consideration its moral significance. Evidence which would be felt to be insufficient to prove the occurrence of a prodigy, may be amply sufficient to establish the objective reality of a fact which is found to answer to the circumstances or conditions of our nature. Nay, more, it may be affirmed that no external evidence alone could ever establish more than an "otiose" belief in the occurrence of an isolated or seemingly arbitrary miracle in a distant age, while the combination of external and internal evidence is capable of producing a measure of conviction which is only less certain than an immediate intuition.

10. But in order to estimate the spiritual significance of the Resurrection, we must first take into account the relation in which it stands to many elementary thoughts which lie at the very foundation of our ordinary life.

God as it is to turn to the light. Reason and experience in each case help him to determine how he shall best do that which he was made to do.

Above all, it is necessary that we should set down clearly what must be taken for granted and not proved: what is the conception which we form of Nature, and of miracles: what are the limits within which human speculation is confined. Till these points are determined, as far as they seem to admit of determination, all further discussion must be fruitless. If, for example, a miracle is inherently incredible, it is idle to reason about a fact which in the end must be explained away. If on the other hand we hold that miracles are, in certain cases, as credible as ordinary events generally, it is necessary that we should show how this belief is reconcilable with the ideas which we entertain of an Infinite God and of the constancy of natural laws. These fundamental questions will form the subject of the Introduction; and afterwards we shall be in a position to consider the Resurrection in itself and in its application to History, to the Individual, and to Society.

INTRODUCTION

Τρέφονται πάντες οἱ ἀνθρώπινοι νόμοι ὑπὸ ἑνὸς τοῦ θείου. κρατέει γὰρ τοσοῦτον ὁκόσον ἐθέλει καὶ ἐξαρκέει πᾶσιν καὶ περιγίνεται.

HERACLITUS.

1. THE simplicity of the Gospel is not due to the absence of difficulties, but to the coincidence of the difficulties which it involves with the inherent difficulties of human existence, when existence is taken as a subject of speculation. Christianity does indeed involve many difficulties, but it does not create them. The difficulties themselves beset us in our daily life (§ 3); but as long as they take a practical form, they receive a practical answer. However arduous it may be to form a clear conception of responsible freedom, we treat others and ourselves as responsible. Christianity, however, which reveals the significance of life, makes us also feel its mysteries. It brings out what was ill-defined before, like the light which does not make the shadows, though they are seen by contrast with it. The truth involved in this distinction is of vital importance towards the understanding of its claims. We are so constituted that we must look beyond and beneath the phenomena of physical life. We *cannot* acquiesce in

ignorance; and that religion necessarily claims our allegiance which answers most completely to all the conditions of our nature. If it could be shown that Christianity introduces some idea into life wholly alien from its common tenor, or assumes principles which we do not act upon, or asserts consequences at variance with the natural reason of men, we might pause before receiving its teaching. But if, on the contrary, its mysteries rest on fundamental mysteries of our finite being; if it takes its stand on human nature as it is and interprets its aspirations; if it carries on thoughts of which we feel the beginnings within ourselves, and opens gleams of hope where we acknowledge that our prospect is clouded; then it cannot but be monstrous to reject it for reasons on which we might with equal justice declare life itself to be impossible.

2. For it is necessary to bear in mind that the Resurrection is not primarily an *explanation* of existing phenomena, growing out of them or introduced to explain them, but a *new fact* added to the sum of human experience. The fact may prove to be an explanation of mysteries which are already felt, so far as it opens a way towards their solution by bringing them into connection with another order of being, but in itself it claims to take its place among the events of human history. Like all historical facts it differs from the facts of physics as being incapable of direct and present verification. And it differs from all other facts of history because it is necessarily unique. Yet it is not

therefore incapable of that kind of verification which is appropriate to its peculiar nature. Physical science deals with law as uniform, and consequently its results can be tested at any moment. History generally records the average results of human action, and its heroic passages are judged by the tendencies which are observed towards similar displays of exceptional power in less moving crises (§ 11). And so the Resurrection, the fact that Christ rose from the grave *and did not again die*—the one fact absolutely unparalleled in itself and in its circumstances—is to be taken in connection with the whole course of human life, and with that instinct of immortality which from time to time makes itself felt with an overwhelming power. Its verification lies in its abiding harmony with all the progressive developments of man, and with each discovery which casts light upon his destiny.

3. It is on this new fact that Christianity first rests its claims. It asserts that the Resurrection is itself a Gospel. For the rest it makes no attempt to lessen or remove the problems by which all life is perplexed. For instance, the existence of matter, the relation of soul and body, the existence of evil, existence absolutely and in time and space, individual freedom and general laws of sequence, are all fundamental and final mysteries from which we can never escape. They are taken account of and dealt with in the doctrines of Christianity, but Christianity does not make them. It will be seen hereafter how they are dealt with, but for the

present it is enough to notice that the rejection of the mysteries of Christianity will not eliminate the element of mystery from life. We are absolutely unable to form a conception of a beginning or of an end of things. The very idea of life involves the antithesis of finite and infinite, and the special difficulties which have been enumerated simply represent the various forms which this one fundamental difficulty assumes when contemplated in connection with the physical world or with human action.

4. This antithesis of the finite and infinite which meets us as soon as we lift our thoughts above single phenomena is the final basis of all religion. It is apprehended more or less sharply in different ages or races, but the essence of worship even in its lowest form necessarily includes the tendency towards a true perception of it. In this respect Christianity differs from all other religions, not in principle, but in virtue of the absolute clearness with which the idea of the antithesis is laid down. The two terms are regarded in their most complete separation and in "the fulness of time" they are combined in one Person. But in saying this we are anticipating what will appear more naturally afterwards. It is not necessary yet to consider *how* Christianity resolves or harmonises the antithesis on which it, equally with all religions, is founded. That which is essential to our argument is that the antithesis itself is not brought into being by Christianity, but is the clear expression of that element in man's

nature, which has sought at all times to embody itself in religious thought and worship—in thought as well as in worship: for the mind which strives to establish its own relation to the unseen by the worship of a GOD, is always led at the same time to ponder on the relation of the World to the same Power.

5. Christianity therefore, as the absolute religion of man, assumes as its foundation the existence of an Infinite Personal GOD, or rather of a Heavenly Father of absolute power, justice, and goodness, and a finite human will (ii. § 2). This antithesis is assumed and not proved. No arguments can establish it. It is a primary intuition and not a deduction. It is capable of illustration from what we observe around us; but if either term is denied no reasoning can establish its truth. Each man for himself is supposed to be conscious of the existence of GOD and of his own existence. We can go no farther. If he has not, or says he has not, this consciousness, he must be regarded as one whose powers are imperfect. It would be as vain to reason with him on religion as to reason on the phenomena of light with a blind man. No proof can establish the existence of that within a man of which he alone has the final cognisance. Practically every one is found to act as if he believed that he had a will, and also as if he were justly accountable for his actions: he is conscious of satisfaction within himself, and awards praise or blame to others; but whether this be universally true or not is of no real moment to us. It

is taken for granted that religion is possible; and if so the conceptions which are involved in the fundamental antithesis on which it reposes are also assumed to be true, though they do not admit of a formal proof. If they are not axioms we claim them as postulates.[1]

6. But though we appeal to the individual consciousness for the recognition of the truth of the assumptions which have been made, the language in which one term of the antithesis is expressed requires explanation. We speak of GOD as Infinite and Personal. The epithets involve a contradiction, and yet they are both necessary. In fact the only approximately adequate conception which we can form of a Divine Being is under the form of a contradiction. For us personality is only the name for special limitation exerting itself through will; and will itself implies the idea of resistance. But as applied to GOD the notions of limitation and resistance are excluded by the antithetic term infinite.[2] For us again infinity excludes the conception

[1] It might appear at first sight that the religion of M. Comte, which is a powerful reality for those who hold it, is an exception to the truth of these statements. In fact it is the strongest testimony to their necessary validity. The "Great Being"—the sum of humanity—which is the object of worship, satisfies the condition of "Infinity" by embracing in itself all the past, the present, and the future in the conception of the worshipper: it satisfies the condition of "Personality" by the concession whereby each worshipper is encouraged to realise the whole by looking at it as partially represented by an individual. On the other hand, M. Comte distinctly recognises human freedom within certain (undetermined) limits.

[2] From this it is evident how utterly false it is to represent the Christian (theological) philosophy of the world as based on the conception of "a world governed and created by wills of which the model

of special action; it belongs to the nature and not to the manifestation of being. But as applied to GOD it is necessarily connected with action and with phenomena, because it is only through these that personality, so far as we observe it, can show itself. Thus it follows that by speaking of GOD as Infinite we simply mean that none of the deductions which can be drawn from corresponding attributes or powers, or the uses of power in man, can be transferred to Him. It would be false, for instance, to argue from the usual sense of the terms employed that what He "does" or "purposes" is in itself bound by time and space. And on the other hand by speaking of Him as Personal we wish to express that He rules and creates as if it were by will, with a purpose towards which all things are guided. So only can we guard against the representation of GOD as the Absolute simply, whether the Absolute be regarded as the Unchangeable which lies beneath the changing phenomena of the world, or as the sum of all that "is."

7. This conception of the Divine Being, which, it must be remembered, is not peculiar to Christianity, except in the distinctness of its enunciation, clears the way to our apprehension of the course and phenomena of nature. For we cannot contemplate nature apart from GOD. But it may be said that such a conception of GOD belongs only to a late age: that the primitive

is in the human will." For the use of the word "will" in such a philosophy is simply analogical, and checked at every application by the supplementary idea of Infinite Power.

notions of GOD are simpler and ruder: that it is unfair to claim as natural to man thoughts which have a limited currency after the lapse of incalculable time. To such an objection it is sufficient to reply that we are in no way concerned with the manner in which the conception has been fashioned. The question is, whether man has gained it, whether he was made to gain it, whether it covers the facts of his spiritual experience? The child includes the man potentially; and the principle which holds true of the development of the individual holds true with necessary modifications of the development of the race. Meanwhile this conception of GOD is assumed, and we must use it. Hence it is against reason to press the results of our observation of phenomena to consequences inconsistent with our conception of His infinite and personal Being. Two errors are specially to be guarded against which are most fruitful of fallacious issues. The one is the transference of the phenomena of succession and gradual growth and slow sequence, which are necessarily part of our observation of nature, to nature as the expression of the Divine will. The other is the supposition that "laws" have in themselves (so to speak) a motive force: that the law, which declares the mode in which phenomena present themselves to us, has some virtue by which the phenomena *are* absolutely; or, in other words, that the Law not only declares how we see things, but *makes* them such as we see them. Each of these misconceptions will require to be noticed a little more in detail.

8. The only idea which we can form of nature, that is of the sum of all phenomena, in relation to an Infinite Mind is as one thought. For GOD all is one and at once.[1] He is cognisant (if we may so say) of things themselves, and not, as we naturally think and reason, of our perceptions of them. He sees them as they are and not as we observe them. Indeed, if we reflect, there is something strangely absurd in applying to the Divine Power conclusions which are based on human apprehensions of things. We must, because we are finite, conceive of things as happening in time; and in the same way we must conceive of GOD as acting, whenever He acts, in time; but it is equally clear that we must not argue as if time belonged really to the Divine relation to the world, or as if GOD acted at this time and that, or at every moment, one *after* another. Any conclusion which rests on this supposition as a premiss is radically false. The statement that "GOD acts" is true at all times in regard to our human conception of Him. We can say justly that He acts *now*, that He acted *then*, and that He will act at some *future* moment;

[1] The reader will be glad to dwell on the thought as it is worked out in Tennyson's noble words:

> To your question now,
> Which touches on the workman and his work.
> Let there be light and there was light: 'tis so;
> For was, and is, and will be, are but is;
> And all creation is one act at once,
> The birth of light: but we that are not all,
> As parts, can see but parts, now this, now that,
> And live, perforce, from thought to thought, and make
> One act a phantom of succession: thus
> Our weakness somehow shapes the shadow, Time.

but when we reason on the human element in these statements, that is, on the temporal limitations, it is obvious that this process of reasoning can give us no conclusion with regard to the action of GOD.

9. Again, a "law of nature" can mean nothing else than the law of the human apprehension of phenomena. We are forced to regard things under conditions of time and space and the like, and the consequence is that phenomena are grouped together according to certain rules. We find that for us (such is the constitution of our powers) the sequence of phenomena is this and not that. Partial sequences are compared and combined, and thus more general sequences are discovered. But however far we may go, we never go beyond ourselves. The law at last is a law for men: its form depends on limitations which are characteristic of men. We have not the least reason for supposing that it has any absolute existence. For to say that things when observed by men will be observed by them under such and such limitations, and therefore according to such and such laws, is obviously a very different thing from saying that such and such are the laws of things in themselves and for all intelligent beings. And if we know nothing of the laws of things in themselves, how can we know anything of things in relation to GOD?

10. From what has been said it is evident that a law, which expresses nothing more than the result of our observation of phenomena, cannot make phenomena

what they are. It is no explanation of how the phenomena came to be or continue to be. It would have appeared to be insisting on a truism to dwell on this, were it not for the general idea which seems to find currency, that when a law (as of gravitation) is laid down nothing more remains to be explained. The law may afterwards (it is admitted) be found to be part of one much wider and more comprehensive, but, as far as it goes, this satisfies all our inquiries. In reality it tells us that something produces results (as far as we are concerned) in such and such a way. But obviously if the knowledge were within our reach our chief desire would be to know *what* produces the results? What brings about the phenomena according to the law? We can show that if a body be projected in a certain direction and acted upon by a central force varying in a particular way it will describe an orbit like that of the earth round the sun. But to go no further, What *projected* the earth? It would be easy to follow up this question by others; but this alone is sufficient to show that in the simplest phenomena we are face to face with a power of which observation can tell us nothing but the fact of its existence.

11. There is then nothing absolute in laws of nature. They are relative to man, and do not explain either the origin or the preservation of things. It is quite possible for us to conceive that the unknown power through which phenomena are produced according to an observed way might have caused them to be produced in another

way wholly different. The belief in the immutability of the observed law springs wholly from ourselves, and is simply a special expression of the axiom that the same power will produce the same results under the same circumstances. But we have no right to assume that the circumstances will always be the same. The range of our observation is bounded within very narrow limits. And yet further, if, as we have supposed, the Divine thought of the world leaves room for the exercise of free human will, it is antecedently likely that we should be enabled in some way to be made sensible of what we call by a figure the Divine will. We may expect from time to time in the evolution of the whole scheme of creation to be made aware of the presence of a Personal Power, not by the suspension of the laws of sequence which we commonly observe, but by the action of some new force. Or to put the subject in another light; as changed circumstances would lead to different results under the action of the same power, so we must allow that there are many cases in which the exertion of the free human will must modify not indeed the Divine action in itself, but the phenomena in which the results of it are presented to us. The building of a city, for example, which depends on the free action of individuals, may modify to an almost indefinite extent the physical character of its immediate neighbourhood, and so more or less of all other districts, in a manner which we can generally follow out; and thus also we can conceive that the natural (though unseen) action of God may make itself felt with varying distinctness in the course of ages, though in this case the law of sequence is undiscoverable by us. At least generally it is undeniable that if we believe in the existence of a Personal God by whose influence we are affected, there is no more difficulty in admitting the reality of His action in various ways and degrees on the physical world, than in recognising it (as we do) in our own souls. Indeed the difficulty in the latter case is greater; for it is perhaps impossible for us to conceive how the Infinite Divine will can act on the human will (as it is felt to do) without destroying the freedom of man.

12. What we can observe of the actual "laws" of phenomena tends in some degree to illustrate the general manner and limits of this modification of effects by the introduction of new forces. It holds true universally that the generality of a law decreases as the complexity of the subject with which it deals increases. In other words, when a result depends upon the combined working of many elements the probability of variation is increased. The action of each element may suffer alteration as to intensity or duration, from causes which are not calculable by our powers of observation. The results of physical laws, for instance, are only infinitesimally modifiable when compared with the results of biological laws. In the former case we can approximately take account of all the interfering forces, but in the latter case forces are brought into play which, as far as can yet be known, escape all individual estimation, either as to their actual or as to their potential

energy. In Sociology this uncertainty is confessedly yet greater. In Theology, which completes the philosophy of life by uniting it with a higher Order, the same progression continues, and it is as unreasonable to expect results absolutely universal in their observed form relative to us in Theology, the crowning science of being, as it would be to expect the results of Sociological laws to admit of a mechanical or chemical or biological expression. Each higher science in the "hierarchy" includes the action of those below it according to their special laws, but at the same time it introduces new forces by which these simpler results are variously modified (§ 26).

13. The same truth may be set forth yet in another way. Even if it is admitted unconditionally that our present knowledge is of phenomena only, it is obvious that the phenomena are of different orders, extending from those which mark the conditions of our observation (*e.g.* time, space) to isolated facts representing the resultants of the action of a multiplicity of forces, which facts, from the nature of things, are severally unique. Some of these may be general: others may be exceptional. In some we can analyse the result and reduce it to simple results of known "laws": in some the problem is indeterminate. And exactly as the subject rises to a nobler elevation our knowledge becomes more incomplete. Completeness indeed is but another name for ascertained limitation. The grandest and highest faculties of man are exactly those in which he most

feels his weakness and imperfection. They are at present only half-fulfilled prophecies of powers which, as we believe, shall yet find an ample field for unrestricted development.[1]

14. In a word, it is evident from the extent of creation, of which we see but the least fraction, and from the connection of its parts one with another, and from the presence about us of forces which we are wholly incompetent to estimate, that we are absolutely unable to judge whether we may not from time to time be capable of calling into action ourselves, or otherwise coming under the influence of, powers which are usually dormant. Every one must have felt at critical moments that he has a fund of physical strength, and also a capacity for moving others by vigour of will, of which under ordinary circumstances he is wholly unconscious. The crisis brings out the gift, and when the crisis is over we fall back again into our usual state. Nor is this the case with individuals only. History shows that there are epochs of extraordinary and, as we should say, who live in calmer times, of unnatural activity and power in societies and nations. A city or a race under the pressure of some great passion works wonders.

[1] The student of Browning will recall countless passages in which he illuminates this truth.

> For thence—a paradox
> Which comforts while it mocks—
> Shall life succeed in that it seems to fail:
> What I aspired to be,
> And was not, comforts me:
> A brute I might have been, but would not sink i' the scale.

Above all, religious enthusiasm, whether in men or in bodies of men, is capable of producing results which under ordinary circumstances would be regarded as impossible. It seems as if the idea of an immediate intercourse with a spiritual world, quite apart from the special form which it takes, were able to quicken man's powers with a marvellous energy and in some degree to work out its own accomplishment.

15. Thus in contemplating nature from its moral side we find ourselves in the presence of two indeterminate forces. Not only are we forced to admit that there is room in the whole scheme of the world (of which we are poor and imperfect judges) for changed conditions which necessarily include changed results; but also we find that men and mankind generally are possessed of faculties capable of vast and indefinite energy. We cannot measure, as we cannot explain, the influence which one mind can exercise on another, or which the mind can exercise on the body. The influence is obvious, but what are the springs and what the limits of it we cannot tell. In such a case even past experience is no final judge. And this reflection brings us to another fundamental assumption of Christianity.

16. Christianity assumes, as we have seen, the existence of an Infinite Personal God and of a finite human will: it claims also to be miraculous. It takes for granted that "miracles" (§ 17) are recognised modes of Divine action. From the conception which we are

necessarily led to form of the relation of Nature to the Creator it has been shown that exceptional action in its course is not only not excluded by the laws which we base on observation, but even antecedently likely. Christianity affirms that this exceptional action does actually take place. And in doing this it only affirms what every other historical religion must affirm; for all alike appeal to an immediate revelation as their original basis. It follows then that all religion which can influence the mass of men (p. 7, § 6) is declared to be impossible if such an exceptional manifestation of GOD is inconceivable or unaccomplished. Nothing remains but a faith which begins and ends within the individual. But not to dwell on this, it is evident that if the claim to be a miraculous religion is essentially incredible apostolic Christianity is simply false. If Christ did not rise again—the words cannot be too often repeated—then is our faith vain. Something may be left—a system of morals or the like—but that is not Christianity. The essence of Christianity lies in a miracle; and if it can be shown that a miracle is either impossible or incredible, all further inquiry into the details of its history is superfluous in a religious point of view. The rise of Christianity will still furnish a historical or philosophical problem of surpassing interest, but the data which it presents will contain nothing on which to found the faith of a world. Thus we are forced to consider whether the difficulties which are supposed to lie in the conception of a miracle are a fatal hindrance to the literal acceptance of the Gospel.

17. By a miracle (using the word in its strictest sense) we mean a phenomenon which, either in itself or from the circumstances under which it is presented, suggests the immediate working of a personal power producing results not explicable by what we observe in the ordinary course of nature. Thus some facts are in their essential character miraculous, as the Resurrection; others, again, are perfectly natural in themselves, but miraculous from the circumstances under which they occur, as the miraculous draught of fishes or, to take a different example, the true prediction of a special event. But they have this in common, that they lead us to recognise the action of some personal power: they involve, as a general rule, an appeal to or a declaration of divine strength. Some facts again, as many of the cases of healing, may be regarded as natural or miraculous, according as we look at them as resulting from powers already existing in man and evoked by special circumstances, or as immediate acts of divine blessing. This indeed is a mere question of interpretation. The principle is attested in a single case. He who believes in the Resurrection will feel no anxiety as to the exact limits within which the divine working is to be confined. Probably he will see it everywhere, and that even in the same sense, for the difference or identity of mode will seem to him to depend on causes which he cannot investigate.

18. From what has been already said it will be seen that a miracle cannot be declared impossible by any one

who believes in a Personal GOD. Nature is the expression of His will, and antecedently to experience we could not have determined that it would be manifested in one way rather than in another. Nor again can all conceivable experience give us a complete knowledge of the conditions which may affect its manifestation to us so as to exclude variety. On the contrary, under particular circumstances which may happen if GOD reveals Himself to men, miracles are as probable as ordinary phenomena under common circumstances. If the result is different, the power being the same, we suppose that the conditions are different; and conversely if the conditions are different, we suppose that the result will be changed. Nor, again, in speaking of a fact as a miracle do we offer any explanation of its being or becoming. The mystery as to how GOD acts is left untouched. Whether He acts as He ordinarily does (naturally), or in an extraordinary way (miraculously), this fundamental difficulty remains absolutely the same. It is neither greater nor less in the one case than in the other. The power which produces the phenomena is indeterminate and indeterminable. Thus while it would be impossible that two and two should ever make five, because the law on which the result depends lies wholly within us; yet it is not impossible that an (unknown) power which as far as our observation reaches has always produced (say) four phenomena of a particular kind, should on a particular occasion produce five such phenomena.

19. Yet further it will appear that a miracle is not

unnatural, that is contrary to and not only different from the observed course of phenomena. It would be unnatural only if it were supposed that the miraculous and the ordinary result were both produced by the same force acting under the same conditions. Or, if for a moment we may use popular language, if it were supposed that the same law could produce different effects. But on the other hand it is distinctly laid down that in the case of a miracle a new force is introduced, or rather, as the source of all force is one, that the force which usually acts freely in a particular way now acts freely in another. That is, to continue to use popular language, the law is not suspended, but its natural results are controlled. The law produces its full effect, but a new power supervenes, and the final result represents the combined effect of the two forces. Let it once be seen that the law necessarily involves the idea of a power acting according to the law, and acting freely, for the law is evidently subsequent to and not essentially regulative of the action, and there will be no more difficulty in feeling that the miraculous action of GOD is as truly natural, that is, in accordance with what we may expect from a consideration of the whole scheme of nature, as His ordinary action. To affirm that miracles are unnatural is to constitute general laws of observation into a fate superior to GOD, or to deny His personal action. And it must be observed that the denial of His personal action in the physical world involves the denial of His action on the hearts of men; for there is not the least reason to suppose that what is seen is less immediately dependent upon Him than what is unseen, or that it can be affirmed beforehand that He is more likely to act on one part of that which He has created than on another. In other words, if miracles are unnatural, then we are hopelessly enclosed within the barriers of material laws and absolutely shut off from all intercourse with the Infinite. But this is against the fundamental axiom of religion.

20. While, however, it is maintained that in this larger sense of the word miracles are "natural," it is necessary to guard carefully against two explanations which have been given to account for their occurrence naturally; and the more so because they have obtained a popular currency. Some have said that a miracle is but the compression, so to speak, of results which are obtained slowly and successively in the general course of things. The water, it is argued, which was made wine by a word at Cana once, is made wine by the vintage every year. The slightest reflection will show that these two processes, as far as we can follow them, have absolutely nothing in common, so that the one cannot even illustrate the other. But even if the parallel were perfect it would be equally nugatory, for in that case it would tend, in proportion to its completeness, to exclude the idea of personal action which is of the essence of a miracle. The same remark holds true of the second false explanation, which is in every way more profound, and even, in some aspects, unanswerable. It is alleged that natural laws, like some mathematical

series, may be intermittent, so that by the action of the same law one result may be given for a thousand (or a million) times in succession and a different result next time. Miracles then, it is argued, may be the exceptional terms of such an order. They certainly may be, but if so their permanent significance is destroyed. Their moral and spiritual value vanishes at once when they are derived from the constant action of the same forces as commonly work around us. A miracle, if it has any real existence, lifts man truly and not in appearance only above the laws of the present general order.

21. It may, however, be objected that this view of miracles as occasional manifestations of the power of God is a conception unworthy of His Majesty: that it represents Him (so to speak) as dependent on time and circumstance. The objection, as far as it has any force, would lie equally against all action of God among men. It is, indeed, a mystery wholly beyond our comprehension how an Infinite Being can reveal or in any way manifest Himself to finite creatures. But in obedience to the bidding of our spiritual nature we have taken it for granted that He does so. And yet further, the invidiousness of the objection lies in the transference to God of those ideas of time and succession which, as we have seen (§ 8), are proper only to men. There is no "occasion" to God. The world and all its history is for Him necessarily one. His action, which we contemplate now in one (general) mode and now in another

(exceptional) mode, is not in itself divided, though we are forced so to regard it. The principle (if we may so speak) which according to His wisdom directs the form of the general action, and the principle which directs the form of the exceptional action, are not separated, so that the one is subsequent to and corrective of the other, but simultaneous or coincident. What is unfolded to us in a gradual process of "becoming" in relation to an infinite mind simply "is." We are obliged to speak of "the purpose of GOD'S will," and so we are obliged to speak of His "Special Providence" or miraculous working; but the original phrase and the adaptation of the phrase to facts are both accommodations; and we must carefully guard against any deductions based upon the human element in them (§ 6).

22. Nor yet again can it be said that material results involve a material cause. We know absolutely nothing of cause. We know nothing of the power manifested in material results (§ 10). And unless we believe in the eternity of matter (which is an absolute contradiction), some material results must have had an immaterial cause. Moreover, we experience daily the influence of will in ourselves, and this is not material. And it has been assumed that our finite will is a real power and potentially free, for otherwise religion is as completely destroyed as by denying the personality of GOD.

23. There is yet another aspect in which we may regard Miracles. Viewed from the human side, when

man himself is looked upon as the centre of the power by which they are wrought, they fall into distinct groups, corresponding to the subject-matter (so to speak) on which they are wrought. Thus man may be conceived as acting upon the external world absolutely, where the general law is modified by his interference, as if he were to walk on water or control the movements of the heavenly bodies: or he may act upon the external world in immediate relation to himself or to those about him, as if he were to modify the perception of external phenomena in particular cases: or he may act upon man directly, either himself or others, as in the removal of disease. Now in the two latter cases an indeterminate element is introduced, the influence of man upon man, or the working of spirit upon spirit and matter in limited relation to itself; and prior to observation it is impossible to determine what varying effects may be produced by its operation. Experience alone can determine in each instance what phenomena may be produced by human will; and the vast range of the power of will, and the unknown depth of its relations, suggest the possibility of an almost infinite variety of results produced by its action under new conditions. From time to time we are startled by occurrences which reveal a power of one mind over another, or of the mind over the body, which seems to be practically indeterminate. In these cases, then, there is (it may be said) a *natural* opening for miracles: they have a point of contact with what we observe in the course of life. So far, then, we must be careful not to lay upon some "miraculous" phenomena a weight which they will not bear. But in the first case, on the contrary, this "natural" conception of a miracle is inadmissible. We can understand how the individual will can affect other individuals upon whom it can work immediately, but we cannot see how it can act upon the external world with which it has, as far as we know, nothing homogeneous, or, which would come to the same thing, upon the universal perception of men. Thus in miracles of this kind we are face to face with a final difficulty, which (from this point of view) culminates in the Resurrection. Yet even here the miracle has a corresponding phenomenon in life. Special prayer is based upon a fundamental instinct of our nature. And in the fellowship which is established in prayer between man and GOD we are brought into personal union with Him in Whom all things have their being. In this lies the possibility of boundless power; for when the connection is once formed, who can lay down the limits of what man can do in virtue of the communion of his spirit with the Infinite Spirit? The distinctions thus indicated ought never to be overlooked in arguments on miracles, but in one respect all three cases are alike. Whether man works upon nature or upon his fellow-men, it is in virtue of a trust in the unseen. Personal faith is the condition of effectual action; and where GOD is supposed to act immediately, the same condition is satisfied in the recognition of His working.

24. It follows that the moral element in miracles is

both essential and predominant. There is always a natural relation between the acts and those for whom or by whom they are wrought. The external phenomenon which would in one age and to one people suggest the idea of the personal working of GOD would not do so in another age and to another people. The effect of the fact, and miracles are always supposed to be directed to an end, depends upon its inherent characteristics and the capacity of the witnesses to apprehend and interpret them. To use a mathematical phrase, miracles must therefore be (generally speaking) a function of the age in which they are wrought. That which on one occasion would be felt to be a personal revelation of GOD might convey an impression wholly different at another. The miracles of one period or state of society might be morally impossible in another. It seems certain that knowledge limits faith, not indeed as diminishing its power, but as guiding its direction. For instance, when any particular physical phenomena are apprehended as subject to a clear law, which is felt to be a definite expression of the Divine Will, it is inconceivable that faith could contemplate an interference with them, not because it would be impossible, but because the prayer for such an interference would itself be disloyal. For example, it would be positively immoral for us now to pray that the tides or the sun should not rise on a particular day. The corresponding act is represented in the Gospels as suggested by the Tempter. There is even a divine "cannot" recognised in the Gospels as well as a divine "must." But as long as the idea of the physical law which rules them was unformed or indistinct, the prayer would have been reasonable, and (may we not suppose) the fulfilment also. We cannot act when we feel that our influence is excluded; and may not the converse also be true? May not all things be possible for us which we firmly hold to be possible, if at least the result would be such as to convey as its whole and general effect the idea of the personal action of GOD? An age records only what it believes; but, in a certain sense also, it does what it believes.

25. These reflections serve to explain the real force which lies in two remarks on miracles which have at present gained a very wide currency. It is said that "a belief in miracles decreases with the increase of civilisation"; and, further, that "our age, in virtue of its advanced civilisation, is essentially and inevitably incredulous of miracles." Within certain limits both observations are undoubtedly true, but the limits within which their truth is circumscribed exclude the deductions which are drawn from them. The sense of the antecedent likelihood of a miracle proceeds from a comprehensive view of all nature, moral and physical, according to the full development of the mutual relations of its parts, as constituting a scheme for us practically infinite. But the necessary condition of all scientific inquiry, and the progress of science is here assumed to be the test of the progress of civilisation, is to put out of sight the indeterminate element in nature, and thus to unfamiliarise the mind with those aspects

of the world in which the miracle finds its proper place. And not only so, but the requirements of exact science bind the attention of each student to some one small field, and this little fragment almost necessarily becomes for him the measure of the whole, if indeed he has ever leisure to lift his eyes up to the whole at all. The more intimately we are acquainted with any one subject, and the more sensible we become of the fulness of thought which it contains, the less we are fitted to take a due measure of its proper relations to other subjects, or to acknowledge practically and without effort that the conditions under which we contemplate it are not in themselves absolute. Thus in an inductive age laws of observation are treated, and with a view to the immediate results which are sought, treated rightly, as laws of nature. If the moral element of life—the idea of personality—be neglected, we cannot of necessity take account of any results which are not entirely physical. For physical students as such, and for those who take their impressions of the universe solely from them, miracles can have no real existence. Nor is this all: not miracles only, and this is commonly forgotten, but every manifestation of will is at the same time removed from the world: all life falls under the power of absolute materialism, a conclusion which is at variance with the fundamental idea of religion, and so with one of the original assumptions on which our argument is based.

26. At the same time such considerations show that

there can be no antagonism between Theology and Science as they are commonly contrasted. So far as these keep within their proper limits they move in distinct regions. Their respective paths lie in parallel and therefore in unintersecting planes. Theology deals with the origin and destiny of things: Science with things as they are according to human observation of them. Theology claims to connect this world with the world to come: Science is of this world only. Theology is confessedly partial, provisional, analogical in its expression of truth: Science, that is human science, can be complete, final, and absolute in its enunciation of the laws of phenomena. Theology accepts without the least reserve the conclusions of Science as such: it only rejects the claim of Science to contain within itself every spring of knowledge and every domain of thought.

27. This holds true of the lower and more exact forms of Science which deal with inorganic bodies; but as soon as account is taken of the Science of organic bodies—of Biology and Sociology—then Science itself becomes a prophet of Theology. In this broader and truer view of Science Theology closes a series, "a hierarchy of Sciences," as it has been well called, in which each successive member gains in dignity what it loses in definiteness, and by taking account of a more complex and far-reaching play of powers opens out nobler views of being. The Sciences of form and number are absolute for man, and have no tendency to lift the individual out of himself. They are purely human and individual. The Sciences

of inorganic bodies add the idea of external imperfectly-known forces to the universal conditions of human observation, and thereby enlarge and elevate the scope of Science while they take away its claims to absoluteness. The Sciences of organic bodies, by claiming to deal with the phenomena of life and will in all their separate and collective forms, bear a wider margin of indeterminate problems and carry our thoughts beyond the region of certain knowledge. The Science of Theology, which is last in its complete evolution as it is first in instinctive apprehension, completes the progression, and by unfolding that which is permanent in life prepares a solid passage from the temporal to the eternal. The individual mind, the material world, humanity, GOD, form the central subjects of the successive groups of Sciences. Each Science, it will be seen, takes up into itself those Sciences which have gone before, but adds to them elements peculiar to itself (§ 12). To the last the laws of each are of full force within their proper sphere, though the results which are properly due to them are liable to be modified by the interference of forces acting according to other laws. And thus in due order knowledge which begins with the knowledge of the conditions of human observation culminates in the knowledge of GOD, a knowledge infinitely less perfect than the former, but at the same time infinitely more ennobling.

28. While, then, we admit that the tendency of a scientific age is adverse to a living belief in miracles, we

see that this tendency is due not to the antagonism of science and miracle, but to the neglect and consequent obscuration by science of that region of thought in which the idea of the miraculous finds scope. And even here the power of general feeling makes itself most distinctly felt against the power of abstract reason. Exactly when material views of the universe seem to be gaining an absolute ascendency, popular instinct finds expression now in this form of extravagant credulity, and now in that. Arrogant physicism is met by superstitious spiritualism; and there is right on both sides. The harmony of a true faith finds a witness to its fulness in this independent assertion of the antithetic elements which it tempers and reconciles.

29. It is, however, foreign to our purpose to consider what may be the causes which impress a very distinct character on different cycles of miracles, and on the form which the belief in the miraculous assumes at different periods. The investigation itself is full of interest, and contributes in a remarkable degree to illustrate the progressive forms of revelation. But for the present we are concerned simply with the possibility of a miracle, which is seen to be included in the idea of a Personal God. Whether the possibility has been realised in the Resurrection still remains for consideration; but the consideration is now open.

30. For if miracles are neither impossible nor unnatural, it follows that the records of them cannot be

inherently incredible. But, on the other hand, in proportion as an event is rare, we are scrupulous in examining the evidence by which the truth of its occurrence is established; and the more so, if the event itself is such as to be easily misapprehended or referred to wrong causes, or connected with false antecedents or consequents. Cases of healing, for example, except under very peculiar circumstances, cannot be alleged as certainly miraculous (§ 17). Other events are unequivocal in this respect. The Resurrection is either a miracle or it is an illusion. Here there is no alternative: no ambiguity. And it is not an accessory of the Apostolic message, but the sum of the message itself (pp. 4, ff.). Its unique character is the very point on which the first teachers of Christianity support all their arguments. It claims to be the opening of a new life to the world. It cannot then be rightly contemplated by comparing it with the events of common history. It is, according to the original interpretation of it, as singular in the history of the whole race of men as birth is in the existence of the individual. In dealing with the evidence adduced in confirmation of such a fact, it is therefore necessary to take into account its relation to preceding and subsequent history; for it may well happen that the presumption in its favour gathered from the preparation which found its fulfilment in it, and from the results which flowed out of it, will more than counterbalance the natural distrust which is raised at first sight by its exceptional character. On a comprehensive survey of all nature, as far as we can judge from the results which are obtained by a faint approximation to such a view, the Resurrection of our Lord, including, as it does, the resurrection of man, may be as natural as events like birth and death, which are accepted as natural, not because we can explain them in any way, but because the range of our experience includes the observation of their constant recurrence.

31. So far, then, we have cleared the ground for our inquiry. If we grant the two assumptions which Christianity makes as being a religion for man (§ 5), there is nothing antecedently improbable in the Apostolic Gospel of the Resurrection considered as miraculous. The same principles which would exclude as impossible a belief in such a miracle as the Resurrection, would equally exclude a belief in anything beyond ourselves and the range of present physical observation. Thus the question practically is not simply, Is Christianity true? but Is all hope, impulse, knowledge, life, absolutely bounded by sense and the world of sense? Is the present and the finite the definite limit (not only of the mode but) of the object of human thought? Is each individual personality bounded on *both* sides, past and future? Is life as well as science *of phenomena* only? Is there no faculty by which man can contemplate the temporal as (for him) a true image of the eternal? Is there no fact which unites the seen and the unseen? Is the spirit as well as the understanding confined by present laws of observation not only in the embodiment of ideas but in intuition? Or can the soul

reach forward to fuller forms of being, not so much future as absolute? Can it, with a consciousness of its divine destiny, look beyond the limits of time? Can it rejoice in feeling what is the glorious part which it has to play in the whole economy of the universe, and regard as its proper heritage a future appearance in the fulness of a glorified humanity before the presence of God?

CHAPTER I

THE RESURRECTION AND HISTORY

Φιλοσοφία ἡ Ἑλληνικὴ οἷον προκαθαίρει καὶ προεθίζει τὴν ψυχὴν εἰς παραδοχὴν πίστεως, ἐφ' ᾗ τὴν γνῶσιν ἐποικοδομεῖ ἡ ἀλήθεια.

CLEMENS ALEX.

1. IT is the common object of all religion to establish or realise a definite relation between the worshipper and the Divine Being whom he approaches. Christianity goes much further, and proposes to reveal the relation between mankind, or more fully between the world and GOD, and to restore the original harmony of all creation. It addresses not the individual only, but the race; its effects are declared to extend not to man only, but to "all things which are in heaven and which are on earth." It is universal at the same time as it is particular. Just as Aristotle taught that the State is prior to the Man, so Christianity claims to address the World while it addresses the Individual, or even more exactly to address the Individual in the World. To use two common phrases, it contains a Philosophy of

John i. 29.

Eph. i. 10. Col. i. 20. Phil. ii. 10. Rom. viii. 21, 22. Rev. v. 13.

History, as well as a Philosophy of Salvation. It disregards nothing in the rich development of human life. It takes account alike of the evil and of the good. It refers to final principles—final, that is, for our present powers—the progress which we can observe in socïeties and nations, and the moral and spiritual education of men.

2. For all creation is progressive. It is a law as well in the moral as in the physical world that nothing is lost. All that has been modifies all that is and all that will be. The present includes all the past and will itself be contained in the future. Each physical change, each individual will, contributes something to the world to come. The earth on which we live and the civilisation which fashions our conduct are the result of immeasurable forces acting through vast periods of time. There are crises in the history of nature and in the history of man, periods of intense and violent action, and again periods of comparative repose and equilibrium, but still the continuity of life is unbroken. Even when the old order is violently overthrown the new order is built in part out of its ruins and not only upon them.

3. The conception of a life of the universe, of a general law which unites and directs the successive forms of all organised beings, is necessarily of modern growth. It could not be formed till History had called

Geology to her aid, and men were familiarised to some extent with the vast space of time covered by the records of the ancient world. Even now the researches of science are far too limited to do more than suggest the idea and mark some salient points in its realisation. Yet it is impossible not to feel that it falls in with our general notions of the working of GOD from whatever source they may be derived; whether they lie in the original conception of a Divine Being, or are suggested by what we observe in the noblest forms of human action. There is something soothing and elevating in the thought of a scheme of Divine government reaching through all time and space thus opened to our contemplation. So far from obscuring the presence of the Creator, it enlarges and strengthens our faith in His operation. It enables us to distinguish between His will as it *is* and our apprehension of its *becoming*. It teaches trust and hope when we are inclined to be dismayed at what we reckon as immobility or waste in the moral world. The sea-worn cliffs, which are once again fashioned before our eyes into records of a new order by the same power through which they were first built up, teach patience with a silent eloquence which would be irresistible if we could enter into its force. Surely we can afford to wait when GOD works thus slowly.

4. The belief in a common life of mankind is of far older date. This is the result of intuition and not of science. It was the teaching of the prophet first and

not of the philosopher. If it was permitted to a later generation to see the pledge of a personal immortality in a covenanted relation which God granted to the patriarchs, it must have been equally clear at an earlier time that all men who are "the offspring of God" were in some degree under His government and working out His will. At first sight it might appear that the spirit of the Mosaic Law was opposed to this divine unity of peoples. But the opposition was accidental, and the Law itself was potentially universal in its promises. The exclusiveness of the Jews was something wholly different from the exclusiveness of the Greeks or Romans. It was based essentially on moral and not on political or social differences. It was religious and not national. The privileges of Judaism were offered to him who accepted the responsibilities and claims of Judaism. The Jew was taught to look forward to the time when all the nations of the earth should worship his God. The triumph towards which he was to strive, was to win fellow-worshippers and not to raise himself as a lord over enslaved peoples. Hence the later prophets were led to regard "the kingdoms of the world" in their relation to "the kingdom of God," of which the Jewish Church was the figure and the seed.

Matt. xxii. 31-33.

5. Something of the same notion lies in the Eastern representation of the successive ages of the world, which was borrowed by the earliest Greek poets, and again adopted by the writers of the so-called Sibylline books

shortly before the Christian era. But the vastness of the scale on which this thought was moulded deprived it of all practical importance. When it was applied to human life it expressed at most the contrast which we find in the New Testament between "this age" and "the age to come." Its units, so to speak, were periods, dispensations, as we call them, and not nations. It expressed a far-reaching faith in the general advance of "the ages" through distress and disorder towards a glorious end, but it had no connection with the progress or development of the "age" itself in which we live.

6. Still, however dim and uncertain the prospect of the life of the world and the life of humanity may have been in old times, it is impossible now to doubt the noble continuity of progress by which both are revealed and characterised; and the view which is thus opened to us of the course of history throws a fresh light on the position of Christianity. It is not an isolated system, but the result of a long preparation. According to the teaching of the Apostles, Christ came when all things were ready and the measure of the appointed seasons was accomplished. Christianity cannot then be regarded alone and isolated from its antecedents. It is part of a whole which reaches back historically from its starting-point on the day of Pentecost for nearly two thousand years. It was new but it was not unprepared. It professed to be itself the fulfilment and not the abolition of that which went before: to reveal outwardly the principle of a Divine Fatherhood by

Acts vii. 2 ff.

which all the contradictions and disorders of life are made capable of a final resolution ; and to possess within it that universal truth which can transfigure without destroying the various characteristics of men and nations. It is then possible that what we feel to be difficulties in its historic form are removed or lessened if we place it in its due relation to the whole life of mankind; and, on the other hand, the obvious fitness with which it carries on and completes a long series of former teachings will confirm with singular power its divine claims.

7. Again: though the birth of Christianity was comparatively late in time, yet in fact it claims to have existed from the beginning as part of the Divine Counsel. We have seen (Introd. § 8) that we are obliged to regard the purposes and acts of God as following one another, though in themselves all the results of creation simply *are*, without distinction of succession. But though the Apostles necessarily think and speak as men, they expressly caution us against supposing that the Incarnation of the Word was in any way an afterthought consequent upon the Fall, and not already included in the Creation. Without touching upon the abstract truth of the absence of temporal limitations in the Divine Mind, they teach, what is in this case the practical equivalent, that "before the foundation of the world" God had foreordained the coming of Christ. The Fall necessarily modified the circumstances of the Incarnation, but the true conception

Col. i. 15 ff.
Eph. i. 4.
1 Pet. i. 20.

of the World and of Humanity becomes first possible when they are thus regarded in their essential relation to the Word, the Son. We do not at present demand more for this statement than a recognition of its significance. At least it places before us what the first exponents of Christianity believed Christianity to be. It was, according to their interpretation, eternal in its essence, as well as universal in its application. It was in itself beyond time, though it was wrought out in time.

8. It follows necessarily from this view of Christianity that it must be placed in intimate connection with the divine discipline of the world in former ages if we are to understand it. As we cannot conceive of the world as abandoned by GOD, and as the coming of Christ is declared to be the complete expression of His love, Christianity must have gathered up and ratified, either implicitly or by a direct sanction, whatever men had truly hoped or learned of Him in earlier times. And this is exactly what our Lord and His Apostles professed to do. They came not to destroy but to fulfil :—to lay open and enforce the spiritual meaning of the Law and the Prophets, in which the Jews "thought that they had eternal life"; and to declare to the Gentiles the GOD whom they "ignorantly worshipped." They appealed to all history and to the experience of all men in support of the Gospel. Christ came, so St. Paul teaches, in the fulness of time, when the due measure of the appointed seasons was accomplished, each of

which was charged with the realisation of some part of the Divine Will. GOD spoke at last to us in the Person of a Son (so it is written) when He had spoken of old time to our fathers in the prophets, revealing His Counsel gradually (in many parts), as men were able to bear it, and variously (in many ways), as they could best enter into its purport. There have been attempts in all ages to separate Christianity from Judaism and Hellenism; but to carry out such an attempt is not to interpret Christianity, but to construct a new religion. Christianity has not only affinities with Judaism and Hellenism, but it includes in itself all the permanent truths to which both witness. It was bound up (so the Apostles said) with promises and blessings by which the Jewish people had been moulded through many centuries. It answered to wants of which the Gentiles had become conscious through long periods of noble effort and bitter desolation. It came not at an arbitrary moment, but at a crisis when "all things were now ready." If it was divine in its essence, it was no less human in the form of its embodiment, and in the circumstances of its reception.

Heb. i. 1, 2.

9. Christianity was connected at its origin with a vast history—with the history of the whole ancient world—and it is also a history itself. It is a history in its fundamental form so far as it is a revelation; and it is a history also in its appropriation so far as it is the informing power of modern society. The doctrines of Christianity flow from alleged facts. The belief in the

historic event precedes the belief in the dogma. The Life of Christ (if we may use this illustration) comes first, and then the teaching of the Spirit. The substance of our Creed lies in what Christ *was* and what He *did*, and not primarily in what He taught. Or, to put the same idea in another way, His teaching was in His Person and in His Life, and not in His words only or chiefly. It is impossible to resolve Christianity into sentiment or morality. The sentiment which it involves springs out of a historical union of man and God: the morality which it enforces is based on the reality and significance of Christ's Death and Resurrection.

10. And yet more than this. From the time of the first preaching of the Apostles, Christianity has been a power in the world acting upon society and acted upon by it. It conquered the Roman Empire, and remained unshaken by its fall. It sustained the shock of the northern nations, and in turn civilised them. It suffered persecution and it wielded sovereignty. It preserved the treasures of ancient thought and turned them to new uses. It inspired science, while it cherished mysteries with which science could not deal. It assumed the most varied forms and it moulded the most discordant characters. And all this was done and borne in virtue of its historic foundation. For its strength lay not in the zeal of a hierarchy who were the depositaries of hidden doctrines, but in the open proclamation of a Divine Saviour. The Cross has remained in every age the symbol and the monument of its power.

11. These characteristics of Christianity by which it is distinguished from every other religion,—that it is historical in its Creed and historical in its development, —even if they are considered only in their most obvious and indisputable form, sufficiently prove that its origin was an event wholly unique and unparalleled in the history of the world. There have been conquerors who in the course of a lifetime have overrun half the world and left lasting memorials of their progress in cities and kingdoms founded and overthrown. There have been monarchs who have by their individual genius consolidated vast empires and inspired them with a new life. There have been teachers who, through a small circle of devoted hearers, have rapidly changed the modes of thought of a whole generation. There have been religious reformers who, by force or eloquence, have modified or reconstructed the belief of nations. There have been devotees whose lives of superhuman endurance have won for them from posterity a share of divine honour. There have been heroes cut off by a sudden and mysterious fate, for whose return their loyal and oppressed countrymen have looked with untiring patience as the glorious and certain sign of dawning freedom. There have been founders of new creeds who have furnished the ideal of supreme good to later generations in the glorified image of their work. But in all the noble line of the mighty and the wise and the good, in the great army of kings and prophets and saints and martyrs, there is not one who has ever claimed for himself or received from his followers the title of

having in any way wrought out salvation for men by the virtue of his life and death, as being in themselves, and not only by the moral effect of their example, a spring of divine blessings. It is of comparatively little moment how and by whom the Christian religion was first propagated, wonderful and exceptional as that may seem. The one absolute mark by which its establishment is distinguished from that of all other systems lies in its very essence. The Gospel differs from every message delivered as from God to men, in that its substance was contained in what befell a Teacher to Whom the Apostles had listened, in what He did and suffered. Christ was Himself the Word and the Truth which He announced.

12. For us Christianity is so naturally identified with abstract statements of doctrine and ecclesiastical institutions, that we are in danger of losing sight of the essentially personal basis on which it rests. It requires an effort to realise with any distinctness the sublime originality of a faith not in the might and goodness and love of a Prophet, but in the inherent power and virtue of the Person and Death of a Saviour. The conception of such a faith was equally novel and definite in the apostolic age. The relation of the Lord to men, viewed simply historically, was set forth as something wholly singular and marvellous. Within thirty years after the death of Christ, if we adopt the most extreme views of chronologers, He was habitually mentioned together with the Father as the source of spiritual grace. We

need only place any other name for a moment in the same position, if our soul does not revolt from the thought, to feel what must have been the intuitive consciousness of a divine presence which enabled the Apostles to adopt such a formula and to consecrate it for universal use. And the effort is comparatively easy for us, which for them (till it was hallowed by some unquestionable sanction of GOD) must have been blasphemous. We are familiarised in theory with the idea of GOD dwelling as man with men, but a Jew had no such belief to soften the awful grandeur of the truth which he acknowledged.

13. Exactly in proportion as we apprehend the exceptional (but not unnatural) character of Christianity, we shall be better able to judge of all the phenomena by which (as we believe) it was attended. If it was—and this cannot be denied—wholly original in its fundamental idea, if it effected a revolution in the popular conception of the relation of man to GOD, if it came to a world prepared to receive but not to create it, if it was bound up with a long anterior history, and has been in turn the life of modern nations, then we may expect to find that the circumstances which attended its origin were themselves also exceptional but not unnatural. The reality of the Resurrection is an adequate explanation of the significance which was attached to the Death of Christ. It seems impossible to discover anything else which can be.

14. Nothing, indeed, can be more unjust than the common mode of discussing the miracles of the first age. Instead of taking them in connection with a crisis in the religious history of the world, disputants refer them to the standard of a period of settled progress such as that in which we live. The epoch at which they are said to have been wrought was confessedly creative in thought, and that in a sense in which no other age ever has been; and there seems to be a positive fitness in the special manifestation of GOD at such a crisis in the material as in the spiritual world. The central idea of the time which, dimly apprehended at Rome and Alexandria, found its complete expression in the teaching of the Apostles, was the union of earth and heaven, the transfiguration of our whole earthly nature; and the history of ancient speculation seems to show that nothing less than some outward pledge and sign of its truth could have led to the bold enunciation of this dogma as an article of popular belief. If, as we have seen, miracles are not in themselves either unnatural or incredible, in this case there is even an antecedent presumption for their occurrence.

15. It has been said, and said rightly, though the statement has been strangely misunderstood, that science can take no cognisance of miracles. Science deals simply with the ordinary working of GOD, with phenomena which experience shows to be capable of being combined in what are for us laws of nature. It represents the power according to its general action

and then assumes it to be immutable. It cannot, from its very nature, deal with exceptions which are so rare as not to be capable of being grouped according to our present knowledge. But while miracles do not belong to Science, they belong to History; and if they are not to be rejected without examination, the simple question in each case when they are alleged is, What is the evidence in their favour both general and special? Is there anything in the character or work of the time which leads us to expect that GOD should reveal Himself outwardly as He does inwardly? Is there, that is, anything which thus makes miracles in some degree natural events according to the larger sense of the word? And then, Is the special evidence for the miraculous fact as clear as we should be content to act on in ordinary cases? This is all which we can require; for the necessary presumption against a miracle, as an exceptionable occurrence, is removed by an affirmative answer to the former question; and religion is essentially a practical matter, or, to express the same truth somewhat differently, it belongs to that order of subjects in which we are forced to trust to conclusions which fall short of complete certainty.

16. The position which the apostolic age occupies with regard to the development of ancient life has often been investigated. Yet even thus there are many points in the historic bearing of Christianity which are commonly neglected. It is true that *we* can see how the lines of Jewish and Gentile progress converge towards

it. It is true that *we* can see how it satisfies instincts which found expression more or less vague in earlier times. It is true that the Gospel was preached first at an epoch when the organisation of society was more favourable to its spread than at any other. But this is not all; nor indeed are these essentially the most important features of the preparation by which the Advent was preceded. If this were a complete statement of the case it might be said that Christianity was a natural product of the concurrence of Rome and Greece and Palestine; that the anticipations of men after periods of eager expectation fashioned for themselves an imaginary fulfilment; that the circumstances of the age offer an explanation of the success of a mere creation of enthusiasm. A full view of the character of the preparation for the Gospel excludes such interpretations of its significance. There was a tendency *towards* the central truth of Christianity, but there was no tendency to *produce* it. Religious speculations had branched out in so many ways that nothing short of the coming of Christ could have harmonised the various results to which they led; but till He came the results were simply conflicting and irreconcilable, and even after He came the solution which He brought to the riddles of earlier life was long misunderstood. Philosophers and moralists had variously discussed the destiny of man and the grounds of right and duty and knowledge, but the debates had ended practically in exhaustion and despair. The records of their speculations show at once their power and their weakness: they reveal what man aspires to know and confess his inability to gain the knowledge for himself. The combination of various nationalities in the Roman Empire necessarily made broader views of the union of men possible; but at the same time the triumph of imperialism tended to suppress every independent power. The material advantages which it offered for free intercourse were more than counterbalanced by the depressing influence of its overwhelming might. The time was marked by the simultaneous existence of countless adverse powers then first forced into contact, but Christianity bears no trace of any temporal or local character. It came as something wholly new to a world whose course was already run. It belonged to no time and to no place. It was a beginning even more than it was an end. And as there are periods in the individual life when the exceptional becomes natural, it may be so with that vast and complex progress of humanity, which we are forced equally by thought and experience to regard under the form of a common life.

17. The very conception of the history of humanity as a life, which is now an axiom with conflicting schools, was due (as we have already seen) in the first instance to the Jews. In spite of the exclusiveness of their national religion they faithfully maintained the belief in a real unity of the human race, out of which the idea of a common life of humanity springs. The Romans had partially witnessed to the truth when they acknowledged the inherent supremacy of Greece in art: the

Stoics had taught it as part of their stern theory of the world; but the Jews held it, however imperfectly, as lying at the very foundation of their religion. The promise to which they looked for the pledge of their divine election extended at the same time a heavenly blessing to all nations. The history of Israel was a continual advance towards the realisation of this fellowship of nations. Each crisis left the chosen people nearer to that kingdom of heaven of which they were the sign and the prophets. And the typical prophet of the Captivity looking upon the great powers of the world portrays them at once in their organic unity, and in the separate completeness of their distinctive energies. In this respect it is of no consequence how we interpret the visions of Daniel, or to what date we assign the book which bears his name. The idea of a life of mankind, of a law binding together different monarchies and states, is there; and from the time when the book became current this idea has been part of the heritage of men. The book of Daniel is (on its human side) the first philosophy of history, even as the book of Genesis is the pledge that such philosophy is possible. The one presents the kingdoms of mankind as mutually dependent and subject to the laws of a common development: the other presents them federally united in "the first Adam."

Dan. ii. vii.

18. The long continuance and varied fortunes of the Jewish nation enabled it to be beyond any other nation the messenger of unity and progress. And more than

this, the purely intellectual defects with which the Semitic character is charged fitted the people to perform this their appointed work. The forms of literature which our western training leads us to regard as the highest, the Epic and the Drama, found no place among the Jews. The free culture of art among them was forbidden. Or, in other words, they were led to dwell upon the indeterminate and infinite, and not upon the fixed and limited in the world. For them all separate histories and lives and embodiments of beauty were incomplete. They were unwilling and unable to see everywhere one formula reproducing itself. The whole history of mankind was for them an Epic, a Tragedy—the one Epic, the one Tragedy, of which the fortunes of generations or families or men were but scattered fragments. They looked upon history as a life directed by will, and not as catastrophes ruled by destiny or phenomena produced by law.[1]

19. Thus it is that the work of the Jews is written on their character. But it is yet more legibly written in their history. It is difficult to say whether their national integrity or their power of assimilation is more surprising. One catastrophe after another overwhelmed them, and they rise the same yet nobler from the fire in which they were purified. The old spirit remained, but it clothed itself in a new form. The

[1] The intellectual contrast of the East and West has never been given better in a short compass than by Browning in a speech at the close of "Luria," beginning "My own East! How nearer GOD we were!" to which whoever has not read it will be glad to be referred.

conqueror lived in the conquered. The people fell beneath each of the great forms of ancient civilisation and received from each the choicest treasures which it could bestow.

20. Egypt, Persia, Greece, and Rome—the great powers of the East and West—contributed to discipline the mind and further the work of the Jews. The hopes of the people were kindled by times of triumph and chastened by times of captivity. A theocracy, a monarchy, a hierarchy, brought out in succession various sides of their complex character and gave to it solidity and completeness. Meanwhile the spiritual teaching of the nation was carried on from stage to stage, so that while nothing was lost which could serve for the training of the simplest, something was ever added which might elevate the faith of those who saw deepest into the divine truth. When the Law, fixed and eternal, failed to satisfy all the wants which were called out by the manifold growth of a high social civilisation, the prophets laid open its inner meaning and drew the outlines of a spiritual kingdom. This new creative period itself came to a close, and the learned diligence of priests and scribes then framed out of the materials which it provided a system which gave definiteness and consistency to the noblest belief of the past throughout a scattered and tributary people.

21. We are often told that the forefather of the Jews was "an Arab Sheikh." Abraham, it is true, was a

Sheikh, though not "an Arab Sheikh," but he was much more. His true representative was not the Bedouin Esau, but Jacob, in whom lay the promise of a nation. The fulfilment of this promise was first prepared in Egypt. Without entering in detail into the various influences of Egypt upon the Jews, we may notice this, the greatest of all: the descendants of Jacob were there bound together into one body by prosperity alike and by suffering. Every power which goes to consolidate and unite a people was brought to bear upon them. The recollection of a noble descent, the consciousness of a high destiny, the presence of a hostile nation, common occupations, practical isolation in life and worship, combined to create and keep alive a feeling of fellowship and mutual dependence among the growing host. The sense of unity and nationality may have been degraded, though it could not be destroyed, by the conditions of ancient slavery. And thus in due time a people was prepared for a sterner discipline and a sterner work. It is impossible as yet to determine exactly how far the form of the religion of Israel was modified by Egyptian influences. But the silence of the Pentateuch as to the future life shows that a power immeasurably stronger than custom limited the character of such a dependence. That which is most conspicuous in the faith of Egypt is wholly wanting in the teaching of Moses. The earth and the present had to be felt in their full meaning. For it is only by looking both backward and forward that the circumstances of the Exodus can be seen in their true light. When the multitude had realised their common helplessness at last the voice of the God of their fathers quickened again the true life of the children of Abraham; and the faith which was called out by the sight of terrible judgments on their enemies, was deepened with awful intensity by a lonely sojourn in the wilderness in the very presence of the Lord their Saviour.

22. The Jews left Egypt a host of fugitives: they entered the promised land a conquering army. But an entire lifetime lay between the two events. A new generation grew up in the wilderness to whom the Lord revealed Himself as King. Henceforth the people never wholly forgot their divine allegiance. They were the people of the Lord even when they most fatally misinterpreted the meaning of their title. The majesty of Sinai rests on the whole of their later history. The sense of a personal relation of each Jew to his God gave strength to the nation and dignity to the citizen. Moses made use, we must believe, of "the wisdom of the Egyptians," of their skill in science, in art, in organisation, even in sacred symbolism; but the constitution which he framed was infinitely nobler than that of Egypt. It was based on the word of God addressed to all: it was free from the degradation of caste: it included the possibility of progress. Egypt made the body of the nation, so to speak; Sinai infused into it its spirit. Egypt united the race: Sinai inspired each man with the consciousness of his own direct covenant with the Lord who had redeemed His people.

Each individual life, in all its parts, no less than the life of the nation, was consecrated to GOD. To realise the kingdom of heaven—the perfect Sovereignty of the LORD among men—was from this time the acknowledged mission of the Jew.

23. After the conquests of Joshua and the first settlement of the tribes followed times of disruption and disaster. The nation was not yet disciplined sufficiently by common trials to trust in an unseen Power. Hitherto heroic leaders had represented to them the personality of the Theocracy, and momentous crises had called out their utmost energy. But all was changed when they once entered on their inheritance. In times of distress they still remembered that GOD was their king; but they forgot Him in times of peace. The lessons of the wilderness were not at once applicable to the course of common life. The people acknowledged a spiritual deliverer, but they were not ripe for a spiritual sovereignty. This was indeed the end of their hopes, but the time was not yet. To lead them to look onward, to reveal the inherent weakness of dominion based on external might, even though the might was from GOD, to prepare the way for another and more gradual training, based upon the characteristic feelings of the nation—in respect of this progressive development the type of all nations—was, as it appears, the use of the troubled period of the Judges. The free uncentralised government, and the movable Tabernacle, showed by no uncertain symbols the nature of

the kingdom which God designed for His people: arbitrary authority and unhallowed sanctuaries showed that they were not yet prepared to submit to its sway. The idea of the Theocracy, if the phrase may be allowed, was presented at the outset of the national life; and experience proved that it could only be realised by a long season of discipline.

24. Thus the establishment of the kingdom was in the truest sense a defection from God, and yet, humanly speaking, it was a necessary defection. An earthly king fell infinitely short of the type of divine government represented by Moses, or Joshua, or Samuel; but he was at once a definite centre and a clear sign of something greater than himself. If he presented the spiritual idea in a fixed and limited form, he also gave distinctness to the conception of the present moral sovereignty of God, and furnished imagery under which the prophets could construct a more glorious picture of the future.

25. The establishment of the kingdom was necessarily connected with the building of the Temple. And the Temple occupied the same place with regard to the Tabernacle as the monarchy with regard to the Theocracy. Both were earthly and partial, though at the time necessary, representatives of something greater and more spiritual. In both we see the attempt to give a limited and permanent shape to that which was, in its original revelation, divine in essence and transitory in its embodiment. But even as God was pleased to

use the monarchy for the exhibition of higher truth, so also He used the Temple; and we cannot see now how the lessons conveyed through it to the Jews and to ourselves could otherwise have been realised.

26. The kingdom and the Temple were destroyed when they had fixed indelibly upon the heart of the nation the idea of the unity of the sovereignty and worship of GOD which they symbolised. The Captivity then spiritualised by the teaching of facts, as the prophets by word of mouth, the lessons which had been taught in a material form. The people came up from Egypt a united nation: they returned from Babylon a small colony to form the centre of a religious commonwealth. A great revolution had been wrought in their national hopes, in their social organisation, in their spiritual creed. They were no longer outwardly bound together by civil ties. Subject to different monarchs, they even served in adverse armies. Their hereditary sovereignty was lost. But political separation did not destroy true fellowship. The unity of a church succeeded to the unity of a nation; and the scattered members of the religious society looked forward in common to the eternal kingdom of a future Son of David. At the same time the service of the synagogues was added to that of the Temple. A hierarchy whose power was derived from education and not from descent, grew up, and more than rivalled the power of the priests. The labour of these scribes witnessed to the cessation of prophecy, and jealously

guarded the heritage which it had left. As a necessary consequence religion assumed a more distinctly personal character. The house of prayer and the skilled teacher brought it close to the home of each Jew. Exile had taught men, when they were removed from their holy place, the full blessing of spiritual communion with God. In the strength of this faith they were allowed to gaze upon the conflicts of good and evil in a higher world; and the enemy of God was seen at length in his personal power.

Zech. iii. 1.

27. Thus Persia wrought out its work upon the Jews, and when the discipline was ended the people were prepared to meet the new influences of Greece. The most abiding monument of the triumphs of Alexander was the city which he chose to bear his name in the border land of the East and West; and the spirit of Alexandria nowhere found a truer expression than in the Jewish colony, which from the first formed an important element in its population. The Alexandrine Jews penetrated deeply into the speculations of Greek philosophy, and their national faith gained breadth without losing its individuality. Nor was the influence of Greece upon Judaism, which was strong at Alexandria, confined to that centre. It was spread from the first more or less throughout Asia Minor and Syria. The policy of conquerors and the instinct of commerce scattered the Jews over the whole civilised world. The dispersion, which was begun on the return from Babylon, was extended. Judaism

adopted a new language for its ancient doctrines. A people who had once been bound by the strictest ritualism within the narrow limits of one land were found throughout all nations witnessing to the spiritual truths which they had inherited and preparing the way for a universal faith. The Hellenists were thus at once missionaries and prophets. They proclaimed a purer creed to the heathen, who gathered round the synagogue without formally taking upon themselves the covenant of Israel; and they lifted the thoughts of their countrymen to the prospect of a spiritual law circumscribed by no requirements of season or place.

28. One special feature of the growth of Hellenism among the Jews demands a passing notice. The spirit of independent thought led to the foundation of sects. The conflicting tendencies which coexist everywhere in religious societies found separate embodiments. Freedom, ritualism, and asceticism found a characteristic expression in Sadducees, Pharisees, and Essenes. The whole breadth and depth of the national faith, so to speak, was tested. Nor was a fiery trial wanting when the elements of truth and error were in danger of being fatally confounded. The Maccabæan conflict restored the Law to its true supremacy, while it left untouched all that was nobler in the lessons of Greek art and culture. A final struggle fixed the limits of the teaching of the ancient prophets, and founded the stability of the nation on the victorious profession of its completed faith.

29. Meanwhile through these vicissitudes of disaster and triumph one faith grew in many fashions and in many parts. The Jews never lost the sense of the blessing which was to come through them to all the nations. Up to the giving of the Law no personal trait of the promised Redeemer is found. Hope was centred in a narrower circle at each great crisis in the spiritual history of mankind, in a race, in a nation, in a tribe, in a family. For the first time the work of Moses furnished occasion to a special portraiture of Messiah's office. He was to be the mediator of a new Law. To establish an abiding covenant between God and man was declared to be the substance of His work. The Law alone was unable to train the Jews to their appointed work. A kingdom was established, and with it a new conception of Messiah was added. The king who gave unity and security to the nation was but a type of the Son of David whose kingdom should extend in eternal blessings over all the world. The earthly sovereignty of the line of David fell. The chosen people passed into captivity, and under the pressure of national disaster learnt from the teaching of prophets to see in their promised Messiah "a Son of Man," who should sympathise with the sufferings of those whom He came to save as well as to govern. Thus the central belief, in virtue of which Judaism lived, was providentially shaped in the progress of the history of the chosen people. Nothing was lost as the conception of the Redeemer was gradually completed. Each period added something which belongs essentially to the fulness of

the conception. And so at last the Lawgiver, the King, the Prophet, the Priest, the Man, are all included in the Christ whom the Gospels present to us.

30. Two characteristic doctrines, which belonged in their completest forms respectively to Palestine and Alexandria, summed up this national belief at the time of the Lord's Coming. The expectation of a Messiah "who should redeem Israel," and the belief in a Divine Word by whom God could reveal Himself to mankind at large. The first hope found expression in a series of so-called apocryphal writings, which generally agree in describing a period of intense suffering, followed by the advent of a triumphant Conqueror, who should bring beneath His sceptre and the Law all the nations of the earth. The process of the consummation is variously pictured according to the position in which the several writers stood. At one time an era of blessing, at another an era of vengeance, fills the imagination of the seer. But the earth is the scene of both. The purification of the soul through suffering, the end of the great tragedy of human life, finds no fitting place in the schemes of outward aggrandisement. "The master of Israel" was startled at the seeming paradox of a second birth. In proportion as the teaching of the prophets was made more definite, its traits were exaggerated and externalised. But in spite of error and prejudice, the hope of the Palestinian Jew was in a Person, a Saviour. The deliverance for which he confidently looked was to be wrought out among men. It was to be historical

in its foundation, and not moral only or intellectual. He through whom it should be accomplished was recognised as "the Son of God," but none the less its end was to be the restoration of the kingdom.

31. At the same time, while this external conception of Messiah was gaining definiteness and strength, wider views of the general action of God were gradually opened. Religious thinkers, especially in Egypt, pondered on the way in which we may conceive an Infinite Being in connection with the finite. The result was a widespread doctrine of a Divine Word through whom God was supposed to be revealed in action and in utterance. In Palestine this Word was regarded chiefly as the medium of outward communication, like the angel of the Pentateuch: at Alexandria as the power in virtue of which a fellowship between God and man is rendered possible. The one doctrine tended towards the recognition of a divine Person subordinate to God: the other to the recognition of a twofold personality in the divine nature. In Greek writers, like Philo, the conception of the Word was further enlarged by the ambiguity of the term *Logos*, which was used to express it. As this might be taken for "Word" or "Reason," so the corresponding idea fluctuated between the objective manifestation of the Divine will and the subjective correlative, whether in the mind of God in which the primal thought lay, or in the mind of man by which he apprehends the revelation. Each varying notion has obvious points of connection with Christian dogma, and just as the Jewish

belief in Messiah preserved the belief in a historic Saviour, so the Jewish belief in the Word prepared the way for a larger view of a revelation of God in man and through man.

32. The two complementary conceptions of a Saviour manifested on earth and of an eternal omnipresent Word thus existed side by side, but they were absolutely unconnected. Philo may have conceived of the Word as acting through Messiah, but not as one with Him. The lines of thought which pointed to the action of a second Person in the Godhead, and to the victories of some future conqueror, were not even parallel, but divergent. It was reserved for St. John to unite the antithetic truths in one divine phrase, which could not have entered into the mind of Philo. "The Word was God, . . . and the Word was made flesh, and dwelt among us."

John i. 1-14.

33. But the preparation of Judaism was not the only preparation for Christianity. In another sense the Gentile world were making all things ready for the advent. The vast monarchies of the East, the intellectual culture of Greece, the civil organisation of Rome, each fitted men in some peculiar way for the reception of the message of the Gospel. The spirit of the East made itself felt directly through the Jewish nation, while prophets yet spoke to interpret its lessons. The teaching of Greece was reflected more or less clearly in the common version of the Sacred Books and in the

speculations of an influential school of Jewish teachers, both in Palestine and in the Dispersion. The material unity and order of the Roman Empire prepared the way for the spread of a new Faith, and furnished the type of a universal kingdom. But it is not our purpose now to consider the relative effects of Greece or Rome on Judaism or Christianity, but rather to estimate generally what ancient life in its noblest forms was in itself as a step in the progress of humanity.

34. Something, indeed, has been said already of the direct influence of Greece upon Jewish development. But the independent progress of classical thought and life had in itself, though indirectly, a more important bearing on the consummation of the crisis of human life at the time when Christ came. In a word, it may be said that the history of the ancient world is generally the history of the gradual separation of man from GOD, so far as the original relation was the groundwork of faith and personal devotion. At the same time the civil power was more and more centralised and offered as the object towards which the highest hopes of the citizen might be directed. The standards which bore the image of the Emperor became the idols of the Roman army; and in its essence the idea of Imperialism is the human antithesis to the Homeric sovereignty of Zeus. It would be easy to trace out the necessary progress of this elimination of the heavenly, externally religious, element from Gentile life in society, literature, and thought. The instinct from which this element

derived its origin and strength could not bear a rigid analysis, nor meet the manifold difficulties of a complex polity. Step by step the patriarchal communities, in which the ruler and the priest were one, passed into the great republics, where a solemn ceremonial witnessed to a feeling of religion, powerful only as an instrument to rule the masses. A single century, but that a century which ranks in the richness and variety of its mental results only after the first and sixteenth, saw the passage from the pious theocratic history of Herodotus to the self-reliant, human analysis of national fortunes in Thucydides; from the awful questionings on fate and foreknowledge and future punishment in Æschylus, which sound like echoes of a Hebrew prophet, to the intellectual naturalism of Euripides; from the rude choric song, in which still lingered some sense of the personal bounty of a GOD of gladness, to the conventional portraiture of an artificial life in the comedies of Menander. The advance of philosophy was scarcely less rapid. The discussions on being which occupied the earliest thinkers passed into discussions on knowing. Aristotle sums up the results of all who had gone before him with stern impartiality, and a school of scepticism followed. Thenceforth philosophy was content to treat of duty and to abdicate the higher prerogatives which it had once claimed.

35. The growth of the Roman Empire is the noblest spectacle of the natural triumph of human power, as it was based upon the surest of human affections. But

like Greek philosophy the Roman constitution contained essentially in itself the seeds of its own ruin. The conception of the family bound together by a common worship on which the state was built, was unequal to meet the difficulties of enlarged dominion. First arose the divisions in the capital itself when the paternal authority of those who had been once fathers in act as well as in name was unable to satisfy the wants of the multitude who had placed themselves under their protection. Next the policy of isolation and civil independence, by which the early republic had sought to keep in contented loyalty her subject states, was inapplicable to the wider dominion of later times. The idea of the family, and with it that of religion, was lost; and when Rome had conquered the world, it was felt on every side that one irresponsible will could alone wield the resources of the state. The soul was gone when the body had reached its full development. Yet even thus the influence of Rome upon Christianity was not less than that of Greece. If the speculations of Greek thinkers had raised problems and fashioned a language which could aid Christian teachers in unfolding the doctrine of the Divine Nature, the determinations of Roman jurists were equally powerful in preparing for the exhibition of the relation of man to God, which was the office of the Latin Church. But this work was still future and unperceived. For the present even the splendours of the reign of Augustus were a sign of failure. Greek speculation had ended in scepticism. The constitutional liberty of Rome had issued in

Imperialism. The promise which the Jew had inherited from his fathers alone waited for an accomplishment, which each change seemed to bring nearer.

36. Thus the fulness and the exhaustion of hope met at the epoch of Christ's coming. The hope of an external deliverance which had been gradually moulded through a long history was waiting its fulfilment. The hope which man had formed of working out his own way to truth and freedom was wellnigh quenched. Old forms of belief, old modes of government, were passing away. It was felt that "the world's great age" was even then to begin anew. Carried away by this belief, Romans saw in the rise of Imperialism the promise of a Golden Age. But the imagery of the Augustan poet, who described the advent of this glorious time, was borrowed from the East, and it was to the East that many still looked for the great Conqueror. So firm and so widespread was this expectation that nearly seventy years afterwards Vespasian was thought to have fulfilled the prophecy by passing from Syria to the throne of the Cæsars. It is needless, however, to dwell upon this instinctive homage of the age to the LORD whom it knew not. It may have been a mere echo of Jewish hopes, or one of those intuitive interpretations of a great crisis which seem to rise simultaneously in the hearts of nations. So much at least is clear to us now, that the Coming of Christ coincided with the beginning of a new life in mankind, with a new development of history which is not yet completed; and, yet more than

this, that the principles of this life are found in their simplest form in the Gospels.

37. Judaism had existed in the face of every form of antagonistic religion, but it had not subdued them. It had the power of life, but not the power of conquest. The life of Christianity lay in progress. It was essentially aggressive and essentially human. Christ was the Son of Man as well as the Son of David. And thus through the Apostles first all the treasures of the East were brought to the Western nations in a form which they could appreciate and accept. The strength of modern civilisation lies in the combination of faith and reason—to use the shortest phrase—which was the issue of their message. The power of their Gospel was felt far beyond the range of its acknowledged influence. The old philosophies were quickened with a new life. Christianity had revealed the seat of their weakness, and enthusiastic teachers endeavoured to supply what was wanting in them. Classical paganism itself was made to assume a new dress, and the bitterest enemy of the faith acknowledged its inherent power by a vain endeavour to transfer its spirit to the polytheistic creed.

38. These considerations suggest a conclusive answer to a fallacy which has come to be regarded as a truism. It is said that while science is progressive religion is stationary. The modes of advance in the two are certainly not the same, but the advance in science is

not more real than the advance in religion. Each proceeds according to its proper law. The advance in religion is not measured by an addition to a former state, which can be regarded in its fulness separately, but by a change: it is represented not by a common difference but by a common ratio. Viewed in this light, we can trace on a great scale the triple division of post-Christian history as marked by the successive victories of the Faith. The fact of the Resurrection is its starting-point, the realisation of the Resurrection is its goal. The fulness of the Truth is once shown to men, as in old times the awful splendours of the Theocracy, and then they are charged to work out in the slow struggles of life the ideal which they have been permitted to contemplate. Thus it is that we can look without doubt or misgiving upon the imperfections of the sub-apostolic Church or the corruptions of the middle ages or the excesses of the Reformation. Even through these the divine work went forward. The power of the Resurrection was ever carried over a wider field. At first Christianity moved in the family, hallowing every simplest relation of life. This was the work of the primitive Church. Next it extended its sway to the nation and the community, claiming to be heard in the assemblies of princes and in the halls of counsellors. This was the work of the mediæval Church. Now it has a still wider mission, to assert the common rights and fellowship of men, to rise from the family and the nation to humanity itself. To accomplish this is the charge which is entrusted to the Church of the Present; and no vision of the purity or grandeur of earlier times should blind us to the supreme majesty of the part which is assigned to us in the economy of faith.

39. It is at once obvious that these great divisions of Christian history, or even, more truly speaking, of the post-Christian world, answer in a remarkable degree to the periods of Jewish history which have been already marked out. The law of progress is the same in both. But if history repeats itself, it is, at least in this case, on an ampler field and with more momentous issues. The discipline of a nation is replaced by the discipline of a world; and (as we believe) an Advent of Triumph answers to an Advent of Redemption. Without following out this parallel further, though it seems to include many unexpected harmonies in things old and new, we must yet notice a progress in Christianity itself corresponding with this progress in its work. The three words which by common consent characterise the great representative churches of the different periods describe the successive stages into which it may be divided, Orthodoxy, Catholicity, Evangelicalism.

40. At first the Christian Faith was simply historic. As long as its work was confined in the narrow limits of the family or of the small communities scattered throughout the Empire, considerable latitude in interpreting the fundamental facts on which it rested was natural or even necessary. The principles of Truth were held firm, but no deductions from them were

authorised. The rapid spread of Christianity through every rank made this state of things impossible for any great length of time. Philosophers became Apologists and reasoned in turn upon the truths which they defended. Yet even thus heresy was long active in every direction laying down false conclusions before the Church assumed the perilous function of defining the Truth. But the work was done by those who by natural gifts and intellectual training were best fitted for its accomplishment. It was the glory of the Greek Church to win the title of Orthodox. But the work of the Orthodox Church, though necessary, was full of danger. There is a strange fascination in reasoning on mysteries. As the argument proceeds men are unwilling to limit their conclusions, and they end too often by measuring Being by our conceptions of it. But yet more than this: doctrine itself is external to us. There is no right doctrine which ought not to affect conduct, but *as* doctrine it has no necessary effect on life: no conquering or transforming power. The effects of a predominantly speculative study of Christianity were seen before long in the character and fortunes of the Eastern Communion. The Orthodox Church is the least inclined of all churches to missionary work. Its part hitherto, since its first great triumphs, has been that of a witness rather than that of a herald. It could hardly have been otherwise. Orthodoxy as such is the translation of facts into a dialectic form; but the life, the power of assimilation and expansion, remains in the facts. Unhappily the Greek Church from the time when its original mission was fulfilled was united with Imperialism. Its potential dangers were thus realised, and Mohammedanism conquered the East. It has been said that the Byzantine Empire died of Christianity: it would be more just to say that the Byzantine Empire sought to imperialise Christianity and perished in the attempt, for Greek Christianity was strong enough only to rescue itself and not the State from the ruins of the judgment which followed.

41. But meanwhile a greater Church had risen. When Constantine transferred the dignity of Empire to his new capital he was unable to bear away to Byzantium the ancient glory and name of Rome. The majesty which had grown round the city during a thousand years remained undisturbed as the prize of the power which should prove worthy to claim it. And the Roman Church was alone able to bear the weight of sovereignty, for she alone had life amidst the shadows which lingered round the ancient seats of honour. From the first, if we can interpret rightly its fragmentary records, the Roman Church had adopted something of the policy of the Roman State. It had regarded ecclesiastical problems from the point of view of society. Its characteristic was breadth rather than precision. In proportion as it embodied more and more openly the style and power of the Cæsars, Catholicity became more conspicuously its ruling principle. Its aim was to incorporate rather than to assimilate the people who were brought under its control. The Republic received the gods of conquered

nations within its Pantheon, and the Church accepted under new titles such popular beliefs and superstitions as could be fitly clothed in a Christian dress. The policy of the Roman Church was to deal with society as it was, and not to rebuild it again from its simplest elements. Thus equally from its position and from its inherent character it became a sovereign power. At Constantinople the attempt was made to imperialise the Church: at Rome the Church became an Empire. The transformation was subservient if not essential to the fulfilment of its work. By the glory of its name and the strength of its organisation it conquered the northern tribes and preserved the treasures of ancient civilisation for a higher use. At the same time it presented the noble spectacle of a universal spiritual power side by side with the temporal power, and independent of it. In these respects its function with regard to discipline was as needful as that of the Greek Church with regard to Truth. But the traditional policy which was its strength prepared the way for its corruption. When the Church became nobler outwardly, it engrossed more completely the devotion of its members, and conversely it became more dependent on popular opinion. At last the Christian was in danger of losing his sense of a personal connection with Christ; and the simplicity of Truth was hidden beneath the accretions of centuries. The spirit of Northern Europe, which had never been completely Romanised, had in the meantime gained maturity, and claimed in the full consciousness of life to hold communion with God face to face.

42. Thus a third development of the Church began corresponding to a new period of life; but it differed from those which preceded by the fact that it was manifold and not one. It was essentially the expression of individual faith and not of common belief. Its ecclesiastical forms followed from the concurrence of private convictions, and did not underlie and mould the societies which arose. Its strength lay in the confident affirmation of two great principles, that the Christian is continuously in direct spiritual intercourse with God through Christ, and that he is throughout continuously responsible to Him for his judgment in divine matters. Personal vitality was infused into religion. Faith claimed the homage of free reason. Individuality was added to Catholicism.

43. It would be easy to point out the weakness of the Reformation in itself as a power of organisation. Its function was to quicken rather than to create, to vivify old forms rather than to establish new. But however we may grieve over its failure where it arrogated the office not of restoration but of reconstruction, it was a distinct advance in Christian life. Where it failed, it failed from the neglect of the infirmities of man and of the provisions which have been divinely made to meet them. On the other hand, the lessons which it taught are still fruitful throughout Christendom, and destined, as we hope, to bring forth a still more glorious harvest. What that may be we cannot as yet know, but all past history teaches us that the power

of the Gospel is able to meet each crisis of human progress, and we can look forward with trust to the fulfilment of its message to our age. The advance towards that perfection of Christian fellowship which we can all imagine, and to look forward to which is our noblest hope, may be slow, but it is slow only in the same sense in which the life of nations is slow. Generations are the days by which it is measured, but in the end it will not fail. The parables of nature are fulfilled in the history of the Church.

Matt. xiii. 31-33. Mark iv. 26-29.

44. The student of history will readily see that the great forms of Christian progress which have been marked out correspond in a remarkable manner with other great periods in art and literature and science. The divisions are neither arbitrary nor applicable only to some parts of human life. The final result of each was a permanent advance, and the power by which each was animated was drawn from the Gospel. If the fact of the Resurrection be in itself, as it confessedly is, absolutely unique in all human experience, the point which it occupies in history is absolutely unique also. To this point all former history converges as to a certain goal: from this point all subsequent history flows as from its life-giving spring.[1] If the Resurrection were

[1] Tert. *de Virg. Vel.* 1. Nihil sine ætate est: omnia tempus expectant. . . . Aspice ipsam creaturam paulatim ad fructum promoveri. Granum est primo, et de grano frutex oritur, et de frutice arbuscula enititur. Deinde rami et frondes invalescunt, et totum arboris nomen expanditur: inde germinis tumor, et flos de germine

alleged to have occurred abruptly in the middle of a series of events which passed on slowly to their consummation unaffected by its interruption; if it stood in no definite relation to the past, as in some sense a solution of the riddle which had baffled exhausted nations: if its significance had not been witnessed to at once by the rise of a new and invincible power which fashioned the development of all aftertime: then we might have paused in doubt before so stupendous a miracle, and pleaded the uniformity of nature against the claims of such an event upon our belief. But now the testimony of nature itself is in favour of the fact. We form our notions of a result from what we know of the conditions under which the forces act, no less than from what we know of the forces themselves. If the force is the same, we are sure that it must act differently under varied circumstances. If the circumstances are absolutely singular in all experience, we conclude that an event will occur without a parallel. If a long train of occurrences before and after lead us to expect that the event would be of some specific kind, then its singularity is an argument in favour of its credibility and not against it. On a large view of the

solvitur, et de flore fructus aperitur. Is quoque rudis aliquamdiu et informis paulatim ætatem suam dirigens eruditur in mansuetudinem saporis. Sic et justitia (nam idem Deus justitiæ et creaturæ) primo fuit in rudimentis, natura Deum metuens. Dehinc per legem et prophetas promovit in infantiam. Dehinc per evangelium efferbuit in juventutem. Nunc (the words admit a Catholic interpretation) per Paracletum componitur in maturitatem. . . . I should despair of rendering the words adequately into English. As a master of rhetorical language the "barbarian" Tertullian has few rivals.

life of humanity the Resurrection is antecedently likely. So far from being beset by greater difficulties than any other historical fact, it is the one fact towards which the greatest number of lines of evidence converge. In one form or other pre-Christian history is a prophecy of it and post-Christian history an embodiment of it.

45. If we next turn to consider the direct evidence for the Resurrection, we shall find in it several elements of singular force. These are the more deserving of attention, because the narrative of the event itself in the Gospels is in no wise distinguished from the narrative of any other ordinary fact which they record. The Evangelists treat the Resurrection as simply, unaffectedly, inartificially, as everything else which they touch. The miracle to them seems to form a natural part of the Lord's history. They show no consciousness that it needs greater or fuller authentication than the other events of His life. Their position and office indeed excluded such a thought. They wrote not to create belief but to inform those who already believed. A knowledge of the chief events in the Lord's ministry, including the Resurrection, and a general conviction of their reality and significance, is everywhere assumed in the apostolic writings. The existence of a Christian society is the first and (if rightly viewed) the final proof of the historic truth of the miracle on which it was founded (§§ 49, 50). It may indeed be said that the Church was founded upon the belief in the Resurrection, and not upon the Resurrection itself: and that the

testimony must therefore be limited to the attestation of the belief, and cannot reach to the attestation of the fact. But belief expressed in action is for the most part the strongest evidence which we can have of any historic event. Unless, therefore, it can be shown that the origin of the Apostolic belief in the Resurrection, with due regard to the fulness of its characteristic form, and the breadth and rapidity of its propagation, can be satisfactorily explained on other grounds, the belief itself is a sufficient proof of the fact. We shall be in a position to consider whether such an explanation is possible when we have examined the form in which the outward record of the belief has come down to us.

46. The letters of St. Paul are amongst the earliest, if not actually the earliest writings in the New Testament. Of these one important group has been recognised as certainly genuine even by the most sceptical critics. No one doubts that the Epistles to the Corinthians, Galatians, and Romans were composed by St. Paul, and addressed to the Churches whose name they bear. Nor is there much uncertainty as to the date at which they were written. The most extreme opinions fix them between A.D. 52-59, that is, under no circumstances more than thirty years after the Lord's death (A.D. 30-33). There can then be no doubt as to the authority of their evidence as expressing the received opinion of Christians at this date, and there can be no doubt as to the opinion itself. In each of the Epistles the literal fact of the Resurrection is the implied or acknowledged

groundwork of the Apostle's teaching. The very designation of GOD is "He who raised up the Lord from the dead." In this miracle lay the sum of the new revelation, the sign of Christ's Sonship. To believe this fact and confess it was the pledge of salvation. On many points there was a diversity of judgment among the Apostles, and a wider discrepancy of belief among their professed followers, but on this there is no trace of disagreement. Some, indeed, questioned the reality of our own resurrection, but they were met by arguments based on the Resurrection of Christ which they acknowledged. Whatever else was doubted, this one event was beyond dispute.

Rom. iv. 24, viii. 11, etc.

47. Moreover, the fact itself was treated historically and not ideally. It was not regarded as the embodiment of a great hope, or as a consequence of some preconceived notion of the Person of Christ. On the contrary, the hope was expressly rested on the fact; and the Apostolic view of the nature of Christ is deduced from His rising again (§§ 57 ff.). In one place St. Paul has given an outline of "the Gospel" by which men "were saved." "I delivered unto you first of all that which also I received, how that Christ died for our sins according to the Scriptures; and that He was buried; and that He hath been raised on the third day, according to the Scriptures; and that He appeared to Cephas; then to the twelve; then He appeared to above five hundred brethren at once, of whom the greater part remain until now, but some are

1 Cor. xv. 3 ff.

fallen asleep; then He appeared to James; then to all the Apostles. And last of all, as unto one born out of due time, He appeared to me also. . . . Whether then it be I or they, so we preach, and so ye believed." Nothing can be more simply historic. What we call the miraculous facts are placed beside the others without any difference. The Resurrection of the Lord, and His appearances after the Resurrection, are taught as events of the same kind essentially, and to be received in the same way as His Death and Burial. Together they formed "the Gospel"; and in this respect, whether it was "the Three," or St. Paul who preached, the substance of their preaching was the same.

48. Of "the five hundred" to whom Christ appeared many were still alive when St. Paul wrote. So too were most of the Apostles, who were their fellow-witnesses, as well as St. Paul himself. Thus we stand, as it were, in the direct presence of the immediate witnesses of the fact. But it has been said that the very circumstance that St. Paul reckons the appearance revealed to himself in the same list with the other appearances, shows that he did not insist on their objective reality: they may have been merely subjective visions as this is assumed to be. The exact converse is, however, the true explanation of the fact. St. Paul believed, and always acted as if he believed, that the Lord did appear in His human nature as really to him as to the other witnesses of the Resurrection. He asserts that all the appearances were equally actual,

that is, external manifestations of the Lord, but not that they were all like in circumstances. There was an objective reality in the revelation of Christ made to him no less than in the revelations to others; but this objective reality was not limited to one outward shape. It was apprehended (as it appears) variously by various minds. Thus we find that the forms of the Lord's manifestation were, according to the Evangelists, most varied (ii. § 18). A marvellous change had passed over Him. He was the same and yet different. He was known only when He revealed Himself. He conformed to the laws of our present life, and yet He was not subject to them. These seeming contradictions were necessarily involved in the moral scope of the Resurrection. Christ sought (if we may so speak) to impress on His disciples two great lessons, that He had raised man's body from the grave, and that He had glorified it. Nor can we conceive any way in which these truths could have been conveyed but by appearances at one time predominantly spiritual, at another predominantly material, though both were alike real. For the same reason we may suppose that the Lord took up into His Glorified Body the material elements of that human body which was laid in the grave, though, as we shall see (ii. § 7), true personality lies in the preservation of the individual formula or law which rules the organisation in each case, and not in the actual but ever-changing organisation, which may exist at any moment.[1] The resumption of

[1] This consideration will help to explain a difficulty which has been felt as to the appearances of the Lord after the Resurrection. His

the Crucified Body conveyed to ordinary minds a conception which could not otherwise easily have been gained, while at the same time it brought the fact of the Resurrection within the reach (as far as could be) of continuous observation. For us the appearance to St. Paul would certainly in itself fail to satisfy in some respects the conditions of historic reality—it might have been an internal revelation—but for him it was essentially objective and outward;[1] and when taken in connection with his life and the other appearances which he records, it lays open something more of the Divine fulness of the exalted Manhood of the Risen Saviour.

49. It is unnecessary to dwell longer on St. Paul's direct testimony to the Resurrection, which is thus carried up to the time of his Conversion, that is, to a date not more, at most, than ten years after the Lord's death. No one probably will deny that the Resurrection was announced as a fact immediately after the Passion. Nothing else will explain the origin of the Christian

dress (it has been said) must have been purely subjective. But a little reflection will show that the special outward forms in which the Lord was pleased to make Himself sensibly recognisable by His disciples were no more necessarily connected with His glorified Person than the robes which He wore.

[1] It is important to observe that on another occasion St. Paul notices the doubt which he felt as to the character of the revelation which he received: 2 Cor. xii. 1 ff. His vision of the Lord was realised under the full conditions of human life: his "ecstasy" left him uncertain as to the circumstances under which he was allowed to hear "unspeakable words," whether "in the body" or "out of the body."

Church. We may go even further, and take for granted that the Apostles who announced it believed in its reality. The life of St. Paul may be considered conclusive on this point; and even if his life were explicable on any other theory than that of a faith which he claimed to share with the other Apostles, it is long since a critic has been found to maintain that the miraculous narrative was an intentional fiction of those by whom it was promulgated. It remains then, if the Resurrection be unhistoric, that they were deceived, and if so, that they were predisposed to a credulous and ill-grounded belief, either by their own character, or by the popular expectations of the time.

50. Before examining whether this was so we may observe how incredible it is from the nature of the testimony alleged that the Apostles could have been deceived. The sepulchre in which the Lord had been laid was found empty. This fact seems to be beyond all doubt, and is one where misconception was impossible. On the other hand, the manifestations of the Risen Saviour were widely extended both as to persons and as to time. St. Paul, and in this his record is in exact accordance with that of the Evangelists, mentions His appearances not only to single witnesses, but to many together, to "the twelve" and to "five hundred brethren at once." One person might be so led away by enthusiasm as to give an imaginary shape to his hopes, but it is impossible to understand how a number of men could be simultaneously affected in the same

manner.[1] The difficulty of course is further increased if we take account of the variety as well as of the number of the persons who were appealed to as witnesses of the fact during their lifetime; and of the length of time during which the appearances of the Lord were continued. It is stated in the Acts that the necessary qualification of an Apostle was that he should be a personal witness of the Resurrection; and St. Paul admits the qualification, and shows that it was fulfilled in his case. Every avenue of delusion seems to be closed up. For forty days Christ was with the disciples talking with them of the things pertaining to the kingdom of GOD (ii. § 18). If we cannot believe that the Apostles deceived others, it seems (if possible) still more unlikely that they were the victims of deception.

51. For there was no popular belief at the time which could have inspired them with a faith in an

[1] It must be observed that the question here is not as to the propagation of a belief in a statement through a large number of men, but as to the simultaneous perception by many of an alleged phenomenon. The former is intelligible even if the belief be in fact unfounded: the latter is not intelligible unless the phenomenon be really objective. In this connection too it is most instructive to notice that the *report* of the Lord's Resurrection was in each case disbelieved. Nothing less than *sight* convinced those who had the deepest desire to believe the tidings; and even sight was not in every case immediately convincing (Matt. xxviii. 17). See [Mark] xvi. 9-11, 13, 14. Luke xxiv. 11, 13, 22-24. John xx. 25. In St. Matthew the promised *sight* of the Lord is the message of joy which the women are to carry to the disciples: xxviii. 7, 10. In St. Luke the contrast between the effects of the *report* of the appearance of the Lord and the *sight* of Him is vividly given: xxiv. 34, 35, compared with 36 ff.

imaginary Resurrection. There was none among the Greeks, whose mythology might appear at first sight to offer scope for its spontaneous growth. But without pressing any particular interpretation of the remarkable words of St. Luke, it is evident from the narrative in the Acts that the doctrine of the Resurrection was the chief point in the address of St. Paul which arrested the attention and excited the ridicule of his Athenian hearers. And naturally so; for while the legends of Greece recorded the elevation of men even to the honours of Olympus, this elevation was effected by the deposition of their humanity. They became gods by ceasing to be men. If the rude inhabitants of Lystra, according to the faith of a simpler age, supposed that "the gods were come down in the likeness of men," in the persons of Paul and Barnabas, yet in this case the outward shape was but a disguise in which it was believed that their divine majesty was veiled and had no essential connection with their nature. There is not the least trace in the popular traditions of Greece, much less in Greek speculation, of any belief in the possibility of the restoration of the dead to the transfigured fulness of a human life. The chief myths which expressed the idea of the restorative power of nature were drawn from the stated recurrence of day and night, or from the annual vicissitudes of the seasons. Their teaching was simply of the inexorable and yet kindly alternations of darkness and light, of death and life, without the element of progress or the transforming change "from glory to glory." Even

Acts xvii. 18, 32.

Acts xiv. 11.

2 Cor. iii. 18.

when the fiction became personal it stopped short of the essence of Christian hope. If Hercules was fabled to have met Death and rescued Alcestis from his grasp by force, or to have descended into Hades and delivered Theseus from confinement there, he is said to have conferred on them no greater blessing than a fresh span of earthly existence. If, after the accomplishment of his labours, he was himself wedded to immortal Youth in the mansions of the gods, it was not till he had ceased to be the champion of men, and had consumed in the fires of Œta whatever showed his fellowship with them. Nowhere else in ancient mythology is there a clearer embodiment of the instinct which craves for a personal immortality and communion with God than in this noble legend, and yet even here the entrance to the new life is symbolised by the destruction and not by the restoration of human powers. To the Greeks the Resurrection, whether as the type or as the spring of a new life, was a strange idea. It included and interpreted their old beliefs, but it also transcended them (ii. § 14).

52. Nor was it otherwise with the Jews. Even among them there was no belief which could have furnished the basis for the Apostolic Gospel. There was, it is true, a popular expectation that Elijah, or some other of the old prophets, should be sent from heaven, whither they had been specially withdrawn, to prepare the advent of Messiah; but this expectation had no real connection either in its ground or in its scope with

the Resurrection of Christ, as preached by the Apostles. It centred in a direct mission from GOD and not in a rising from the grave to a new life: it culminated in the accomplishment of a work among men, and not in the elevation of humanity to heaven. After the death of John the Baptist, again, some said "that he was risen from the dead" when they heard of the works of Christ; but this was simply the interpretation of a report in connection with the opinion that John was indeed "Elias." Nothing was based upon the conjecture. Others, again, in the course of the Lord's ministry were, according to the Evangelists, restored to life; but this restoration was to a mortal and not to an immortal life. Such a resurrection, so far from being a parallel to the Resurrection of Christ, is the very opposite to it. The belief in the resuscitation of the dead to the vicissitudes of ordinary life would indispose for the belief in a rising to a life wholly new in kind and issue. And such is the life of the Risen Lord which is portrayed in the Gospels. Thus while we admit all the records of resuscitation contained in the Scriptures, there is absolutely not the slightest anticipation in earlier history of such a Resurrection as that of Christ. The conception as expressed by the Evangelists and Apostles has itself the characteristics of a Revelation (compare ii. § 16).

53. But it may be said that the idea was included in that of Messiah. There were, it is true, very vivid anticipations of a coming Messiah, of some triumphant King who should restore the old glories of the house of

David, but the path which was marked out for Him by common consent was that of victory, and not of defeat and death. There is no evidence that the Jews in our Lord's time had formed any conception of a suffering Messiah. If Christ spoke of His Passion as the Son of Man, they could only ask with wonder, Who this Son of Man was? If the prophet described a deliverer, despised and afflicted, the question rose to their lips whether "he spoke of himself or some other." And if the idea of Messiah's death was unknown, so also was that of the Resurrection, which is the complement of it.

John xii. 34.

Acts viii. 34.

54. Nor were the disciples in this respect more far-seeing or better instructed than their countrymen. On this point the Gospels are an unexceptionable authority; and nothing is more striking than the apparent inability of the Apostles, who were nearest to the Lord, to lay aside the hopes in which they had been reared. When the Lord was raised from the dead they understood at last what He had said to them, but not before. The thought of His death was one which they felt ought to be cast aside as a temptation to distrust. And when at last He died, their hope was gone. There is not a word to indicate that this catastrophe led them to any truer view of His work. Those who loved Him most devotedly came to embalm His corpse. The first tidings of His Resurrection seemed as "idle talk"; and the Evangelists paint in vivid colours, the strangeness of which proves

Matt. xvi. 21-23.

Luke xxiv. 21.

them to be faithful, "the slowness" and "hardness of heart," which hindered the disciples from believing a fact which brought with it a revolution of their ancient faith.

55. But the revolution was accomplished. If we compare the portraiture of the Apostles as given in St. Luke's Gospel with that in his book of the Acts, we cannot but feel that we are looking on the same men, but transfigured in the latter case by the working of some mighty influence. There are the old traits of individuality, but they are ennobled. The relation in which the disciples stand to their Lord is not less personal, but it is less material. He is regarded as their Saviour as well as their Teacher. What was before vague and undecided is defined and organised. Those who when Christ was yet with them wavered in spite of their love for Him, mistook His words, misunderstood His purpose, forsook Him at His Passion, after a brief interval court danger in the service of a Master no longer present, proclaim with unfaltering zeal a message hitherto unheard, build up a society in faith on His Name, extend to Samaritans and Gentiles the blessings which were promised to the people of God. However we explain it, the change is complete and certain. Their whole moral nature was transformed. As far as we can see there was no spring of hope within them which could have had such an issue. The anticipations which they shared with their countrymen and those which the immediate presence of Christ had awakened, were dissi-

pated by His Death. Whatever new impulse moved and animated them must have been from without, clear, and powerful. It must have been clear, to make itself felt to men who were in no way predisposed to yield to it: powerful, to remould once and for ever their notions of the work of Messiah. The Resurrection satisfies both conditions. As a fact with which the disciples were familiarised by repeated proofs, it was capable of removing each lingering doubt: as a Revelation of which the meaning was finally made known by the withdrawal of Christ from the earth, it opened a new region and form of life, the apprehension of which would necessarily influence all their interpretations of the Divine promises. If the crucified Lord did rise again, we can point to effects which answer completely to what we may suppose to have been the working of the stupendous miracle on those who were the first witnesses of it: if He did not, to what must we look for an explanation of phenomena for which the Resurrection is no more than an adequate cause?

56. In nothing is the spiritual transformation of the Apostles more striking than in their view of the Person of Christ. The words in which He spoke of the atonement which He should make necessarily fell unheeded by those who could not realise the fitness of His Death. There is nothing in the Gospels (and for this we may fairly quote them) to show that personal deliverance from sin and corruption—the transfiguration of all man's natural powers—was ever connected with His

work during His lifetime by those who heard Him.[1] "These things," it is emphatically said, "understood not His disciples at the first." He received sinners, it is true, but it was not felt that their restoration was a type of the restoration of all men. Still less, if possible, is there any indication that the Apostles understood before the Resurrection that the Blood of Christ should ratify a new covenant to be embodied in a Universal Church. The meaning of the Last Supper was hidden from them, as subsequent events showed, till after the Lord's Death. But then, from some source or other, a flood of light is seen to have been poured on all which they had regarded before with silent and hesitating wonder. The first invitation which they addressed to those who had joined in the Crucifixion was "to be baptized in the name of Jesus Christ for the remission of sins." The day of Pentecost sealed the testimony of Easter. And from that time forth union with Christ by baptism was the first condition of Apostolic fellowship. His Name was declared to be the only "name under heaven given among men whereby we must be saved." His Passion was acknowledged as part of the divine counsel. His Return was set forth as the certain object of the believer's hope. Nor are we left in doubt as to the power which had wrought the change. The ground on which the Apostles rested their appeal was

John xii. 16. Luke xviii. 34.

Acts ii. 38.

Acts iv. 12.

[1] The inspired confession of St. Peter, John vi. 68, is the nearest approach to a direct recognition of this Truth which the Lord taught (Matt. xx. 28), but in this respect it may be compared with the use of the corresponding passage in Acts v. 20.

the Resurrection: the function which they claimed for themselves was to bear witness to it. Their belief was not an idle assent, but the spring of a new life. And the belief itself was new in kind. It was not like that affectionate credulity with which an oppressed state or party believes in the reappearance of a lost leader. It was a confession of error before it was an assertion of faith. It involved a renunciation of popular dogmas in which those who held it had been reared. It proclaimed a truth altogether new and unlike any which men had held before (§§ 51 f.). If ever the idea of delusion can be excluded, it must be in a case when it is alleged to explain a conviction which transformed at once the cherished opinions of a large body of men of various characters and powers, and forced them to a painful and perilous work for which outwardly they had no inclination or advantages.

57. If we look a little deeper at the Apostolic faith we shall feel still more strongly the effect of the belief in the Resurrection. To do this we must turn to the Epistles of St. Paul, as the earliest memorials of Christian teaching addressed to Christians; for hitherto we have noticed only the simple message addressed to mixed and unbelieving hearers. In many respects, as we might naturally expect, there is a wide difference between the contents of these two forms of the Gospel; but their groundwork is identical. The fuller and more developed doctrine of St. Paul is as essentially historical as the first address of an Evangelist to Jews or Gentiles.

This has been pointed out already (§§ 45 ff.); but one most important element of faith which St. Paul brings out from the history remains yet to be considered. In the first addresses of the Apostles reported in the Acts the Death of Christ is treated rather as a difficulty to be explained than as a spring of blessing. If we realise the circumstances under which they spoke, it could not be otherwise, and this peculiarity alone justifies us in assuming that the narrative is in the main authentic. But St. Paul, in writing to Christians (and no less in speaking to Christians), treats this fact very differently. The Death of Christ—the mode and the issue of that Death—is the centre round which all his doctrine turns; for to the Christian the Death of Christ involves the Resurrection. "I determined not to know anything among you," he says to the Corinthians, "save Jesus Christ, and Him crucified." "God forbid," he writes in another place, "that I should glory, save in the cross of our Lord Jesus Christ." And the reason is obvious; since the Death of Christ for the Christian includes the whole mystery of the Redemption. The Resurrection is necessarily involved in it when we acknowledge that He who died was the Son of God. Thus the great Epistles to which we confine ourselves abound with such passages as the following: "Christ gave Himself for our sins." "We are not our own: we were bought with a price." "If one died for all, then all died. . . . Behold all things have become new. But all things are of God, who

e.g. Acts xx.

1 Cor. ii. 2.

Gal. vi. 14.

Gal. i. 4.

1 Cor. vi. 20.

2 Cor. v. 15, 18.

reconciled us to Himself through Jesus Christ." "God commendeth His love towards us, in that while we were yet sinners, Christ died for us. Much more then, being now justified by His blood, we shall be saved from wrath through Him."

Rom. v. 8, 9.

58. With these passages are connected others which present the same truth of the restoration of unity to humanity in the Risen Christ in different points of view. Thus: "To us there is one God, the Father, of Whom are all things, and we unto Him; and one Lord Jesus Christ, through Whom are all things, and we through Him." And again: "We being many, are one body in Christ, and every one members one of another." We "are all the children of God by faith in Christ Jesus. . . . There can be neither Jew nor Greek, there can be neither bond nor free, there can be no male and female: for (we) are all one man (εἷς) in Christ Jesus." Or, in other words, Christ, as He is revealed to us, in His Life, His Death, His Resurrection, is the One Mediator by Whom every blessing comes; the one all-containing Presence by Whom men are bound together. In His Person every difference of race, of station, of nature, is done away. "In Christ," to use the favourite phrase of the Apostle, our whole life and being and work are centred.

1 Cor. viii. 6.

Rom. xii. 5.

Gal. iii. 26, 28.

59. Long familiarity with such words has made it very difficult for us to realise the magnitude of the

revelation which they convey. The fitness of the doctrine to satisfy the wants of men makes us inclined to believe that it is natural. But if we place on the one side the outward circumstances of Christ's Death, and on the other these interpretations of its significance: if we measure what seemed to be the hopeless ignominy of the catastrophe by which His work was ended, and the Divine prerogatives which are claimed for Him, not in spite of, but in consequence of that suffering of shame; we shall feel the utter hopelessness of reconciling the fact and the triumphant deduction from it without some intervening fact as certain as Christ's Passion and glorious enough to transfigure its sorrow. For we must ever bear in mind that the Apostles do not deal with abstract doctrine, but with doctrine centred in facts. They do not teach a redemption to be wrought out by each man for himself, after the example of Christ, but of redemption wrought for each by Christ, and placed within their reach. They do not teach merely an original union of men, but a spiritual union accomplished in the Person of Christ. They do not teach a liberty which sets aside the distinctions and duties of society, but a liberty which springs from the transformation of every claim of life into a spontaneous act of filial love through the revelation of the Father in His Son. They do not teach an immortality of the soul as a consequence flowing from any conceptions of man's essential nature, but a resurrection of the body not only historically established in the rising again of Christ, but given to us through Him

1 Cor. xv. 45 ff.

who is "the Resurrection and the Life." If Christ rose, to repeat the alternative which we have proposed before, all this is intelligible. The miracle was as a new-birth of humanity. If Christ did not rise, we have not only to explain how the belief in His Resurrection came to be received without any previous hopes which could lead to its reception, but also how it came to be received with that intensity of personal conviction which could invest the Life and Person of Christ with attributes never before assigned to any one, and that by Jews, who had been reared in the strictest monotheism.

60. There is yet one other aspect in which we may see the power of the early faith in the Resurrection. Next to the fact that Christ rose from the dead, the topic most frequently insisted on in the Apostolic writings is that He will come again from heaven. It would be out of place to discuss the form which this belief took, or the interpretation of the passages of the Epistles in which it is enforced. One point only may be noticed. The material imagery in which the belief was popularly embodied shows in what sense the Resurrection itself was understood. In proportion as the Return of Christ was apprehended in a definite outward shape, so also must His Departure have been held to have taken place in the same manner. The two events are completely correlative. And upon reflection it will be felt that the expectation of the Return was in itself exceptional and in need of explanation. It has frequently happened that

nations have looked for the restoration of the hero-king in whom they had seen the pledge of unaccomplished triumphs. But in each case the hope was based on the denial of death. The hero was sleeping like Arthur in the deep shades of Avalon, or like Barbarossa in some subterranean cavern; or he was withdrawn for a time like Harold in the recesses of a cloister, or like Don Sebastian in obscure captivity; but the devotion of his people would not believe that he was dead. That alone was impossible: against that supreme issue popular faith knew no availing power. But it was quite otherwise with the belief of Christians. The Death of their Lord was as much a part of their Gospel as His Resurrection. Nay, more, His Exaltation was in one aspect a consequence of His Death. Thus if the early looking for Christ has any point of contact with the instinctive expression of national love, it is essentially distinguished from it in the circumstances of its origin. Such a fact as the Resurrection intervening between the Passion and the Return explains adequately, as it appears nothing else could do, the confident expectation of Christ's Second Coming in the mode in which the early Christians looked for it.

Phil. ii. 6-11.

61. The same also may be said of the Apostolic interpretation of the Sacraments. It has been frequently argued that the Christian doctrine of the Sacraments corresponds with the Christian doctrine of the Incarnation. It could be shown that it is equally closely connected, though the correspondence is necessarily less

complete, with the fact of the Resurrection. But it does not fall within our scope to examine the essential conception of a Sacrament. It is enough to observe that the external forms in which the conception was realised witness to the transforming power of the belief in the fact of Christ's rising again. The belief in the Resurrection, which was the groundwork of the Church, penetrated every part of its faith and worship. The earliest Christians kept "the eighth day for joy, as that on which Jesus rose from the dead"; . . . and the two rites which were of universal observance commemorated not obscurely the same central fact. The celebration of the Holy Eucharist is absolutely unintelligible without faith in a risen Saviour. "As often as ye eat this bread and drink this cup, ye do show the Lord's death till He come." The rite was not a memorial of death simply, but of death conquered by life. The seal of the efficacy of the death of Christ was given in the Resurrection; and the limit of the commemoration of His Passion was looked for in His Return. Baptism, again, was regarded as embodying the teaching of the same facts: "We were buried with Him by baptism unto death: that like as Christ was raised up from the dead by the glory of the Father, even so we also should walk in newness of life." So thoroughly was the faith in the Resurrection of Christ inwrought into the mind of the first Christians that the very entrance into their society was apprehended under the form of a resurrection. The fact was not an article of their creed, but

Barn. *Ep.* 15.

1 Cor. xi. 26.

Rom. iv. 25.

Rom. vi. 4.

the life of it. It was confessed in action as well as in word. And no evidence of the power or reality of a belief can be less open to suspicion than that which is derived from public services, which, as far as all evidence reaches, were contemporaneous with its origin and uninterruptedly perpetuated throughout the body which holds it.

62. Thus the continuity of the life of the Christian Church is itself, when viewed in this light, a substantial proof of the reality of the fact on which it was established. Other religions have been powerful and lasting in virtue of the partial truths which they enshrined and offered to the devotion of believers. But in Christianity, if we regard the claims on which it was first accepted and through which it has at all times exercised its characteristic power, no such partiality is possible. It professes to bring a new life to light. It is a subordinate though yet a necessary part of its working that it illuminates the past. Christ is presented to us not simply as the Guide of men, but as the Way. The Apostles preach not only that men may be united to God, but *how* they may be united to Him. Every precept of Christianity is quickened by the power of the Death and Resurrection of Christ. It is by the presence of this power that they are Christian; and it is as Christian that they conquer the world. Nothing could show a more profound misapprehension of the Gospel than to substitute the name Catholicity for Christianity in the estimate of its social and political work. Its

essence lies in the exhibition of a personal Saviour. "If thou shalt confess with thy mouth 'Jesus is Lord,' and shalt believe in thine heart that GOD raised Him from the dead, thou shalt be saved." From this confession and this faith spring directly the various organisations of the Church which have found acceptance at different times and under different circumstances. The one fact of the Resurrection underlies them all, and when divorced from it they lose their vitality (Introd. § 16). This being so it is impossible to exaggerate the importance of a living apprehension of the Resurrection as the Apostles announced it. It is not, as we have seen, taken out of the range of possible facts by any antecedent considerations; and, as it seems, no other evidence in its favour consistent with its character as the basis of a religion at once historical and spiritual, could have been more complete than that which still lies within our reach.

Rom. x. 9.

63. To sum up briefly what has been said. It has been shown that the Resurrection is not an isolated event in history, but at once the end and the beginning of vast developments of life and thought; that it is the climax of a long series of Divine dispensations which find in it their complement and explanation; that it has formed the starting-point of all progressive modern societies, ever presenting itself in new lights according to the immediate wants of the age. It has been shown that in the character of the fact there is nothing which can appear incredible or, in such a con-

nection, even improbable to any one who believes in a Personal God. It has been shown that the direct evidence for the event is exactly of the same kind which we have for the other events in the Life of Christ; that St. Paul appeals to his own experience and to the experience of the Apostles for the certainty of its literal accomplishment; that it is incontestable that the Apostles acted from the first as if they believed it, and that their sincerity cannot be doubted; that the nature of the outward proof alleged seems to render it impossible that they could have been victims of a delusion; that the substance of their belief was something wholly novel, removed equally from the belief in a fantastic vision, and from the belief in a restoration to a corruptible life; that the effects of it upon themselves were such that the conviction must (so to speak) have been forced upon them by overwhelming power, capable of changing their personal character, of transforming their hereditary faith, of inspiring them with new thoughts and hopes; that the Christian Church was founded upon the belief, and embodied it in rites coeval with its foundation. Nothing has been said of the testimony of St. John, and St. Peter, and the first three Evangelists, lest exception might be taken to their authority. Every conclusion has been rested upon documents which criticism has never assailed. But at this point we may take account of the evidence from other sources. The common contents of the Synoptic Gospels can be shown (I believe) to be anterior to the Epistles of St. Paul, and to contain the sum of the earliest Apostolic preaching in Judæa; if this be so we have in them the testimony not of one witness only, but the common testimony of most of those who saw the Lord after He rose again. The authenticity of the first Epistle of St. Peter cannot be questioned without the most arbitrary neglect of external evidence, and in that the Apostle to whom Christ first showed Himself speaks of Him as "fore-ordained before the foundation of the world, but (made) manifest in these last times for (those) who by Him do believe in God, that raised Him up from the dead, and gave Him glory; that (their) faith and hope might be in God." The Gospel of St. John, again, seems to me to be an indubitable work of the disciple whom Jesus loved; and after recounting some of the appearances of the Lord after His Resurrection, the Evangelist completes his Gospel, as it stood originally, with the words: "Many other signs truly did Jesus in the presence of His disciples, which are not written in this book; but these are written, that ye might believe that Jesus is the Christ, the Son of God, and that believing ye might have life in His name."

1 Peter i. 20, 21.

John xx. 30, 31.

Indeed, taking all the evidence together, it is not too much to say that there is no single historic incident better or more variously supported than the Resurrection of Christ. Nothing but the antecedent assumption that it must be false could have suggested the idea of deficiency in the proof of it. And it has been shown that when it is considered in its relation to the whole revelation of which it is a part, and to the conditions of the Divine action, which we have assumed, this miraculous event requires a proof in no way differing in essence from that on which the other facts with which it is associated are received as true. In a word, the circumstances under which God is said to have given a revelation to men in the Resurrection of the Lord Jesus were such as to make the special manifestation of power likely or even natural; and the evidence by which the special Revelation is supported is such as would in any ordinary matter of life be amply sufficient to determine our action and belief.

If we next turn from history to the Individual man, it will appear that the Resurrection throws as much light on the mysteries of personal life as it does on the whole progress of mankind.

CHAPTER II

THE RESURRECTION AND MAN

C'est un des grands principes du Christianisme, que tout ce qui est arrivé à JESUS-CHRIST doit se passer dans l'âme et dans le corps de chaque Chrétien. PASCAL.

1. HITHERTO we have considered the Resurrection simply as a fact, the central point of universal history, the outward cause of revolutions in thought and in society. It still remains to analyse the essential meaning of the fact in reference to the individual, to discover, if it may be, what are the special lessons as to our nature and destiny of the Revelation which it contains. Some of these we have indeed already touched on in considering the views of our Lord's Person and Work which were presented by the Apostles after He rose from the dead (i. §§ 55 ff.). But we may go yet further, and consider the relation of the Resurrection, accepted as a fact, to some of the great problems of life, apart from the earliest historical interpretation of its teaching.

2. That we may do this in any way satisfactorily, it is necessary that we should go back for a moment to

take account of the simplest elements to which the questions which are involved in the discussion can be reduced. It appears, then, that we are conscious of three distinct existences—Self, the World (that is, a limited "*Not-I*"), and God. We cannot prove the reality of these existences as we have already seen (Introd. § 4); but, on the other hand, in some form or other all our life testifies to our conviction that they *are*. It is impossible to hold that Self is the only true being or self-existent: it is equally impossible to hold that Self is the only manifestation of the Being on which it depends. Thus we are forced to accept that mystery as final, which represents as essentially distinct, yet for us in inseparable juxtaposition, on one side the Creator, on the other Creation, of which the individual "*I*" is a part.

3. The suppression of any one of these elements necessarily involves an essentially imperfect and therefore a false view of the Universe, and every age offers types of the errors which thus arise. Some speculators neglect the free power of the human will. Man is, according to this view, only a piece of mechanism which responds completely to the forces which act upon it; but in himself he has no originative power of thought or action. The result is Fatalism, which is logically unassailable and yet known instinctively to be untrue. Others, again, with a nobler aspiration reduce life to a personal relation between man and his Creator. For them the world vanishes before this awful fellowship, and finds no place in their scheme of existence. So

mysticism arises, which with all its holy power yet does violence to the conditions of life, and neglects some of its richest resources and most certain safeguards against fatal error. Then comes a reaction, and a third school possessed by the fulness of earthly existence refuse to look beyond it. For them GOD lies wholly beyond the region of knowledge. But the conscience of man triumphs over material Positivism and claims a religion, which by a strange irony is offered in a shape most akin to Fetishism. Thus humanity rejects each imperfect system, which severally, as systems, are irrefragable; and waits patiently for that completer wisdom which shall harmonise the present contradictions of the full view of life.

4. If, then, we look outside ourselves there is an antithesis which cannot be reduced. If, again, we look at that which we each call *I*, it will be seen to be essentially twofold. There is an organism, and something which acts through the organism. There is a unity of will with a multiplicity of functions. There is an element of permanence in the midst of constant change. There are laws, and a power which makes itself felt in accordance with these laws. The organism, with all its variety of sense, its capacity for service, its laws of decay and assimilation, we call the body: the self-moving power, which originates and controls action, we call the soul. And this twofold being is naturally influenced by a twofold affinity. On the one side, through the "body," it is connected with the world: on

the other, through the "soul" (the "spirit"), with GOD. Or, in other words, the body is inherently finite, the soul aspires at least towards the infinite. Thus recurring to what has been already said (§ 2) we see that consciousness reveals to us in ourselves individually a fundamental antithesis corresponding to the antithesis which we are forced to recognise without us.

5. Yet more: the *I* consists in this antithesis. Nothing is more common than to hear it assumed that the "soul" is the real self. Yet nothing can be more clear upon reflection than that the only "self" of which we are conscious is made up of "soul" and "body." The workings of these two are absolutely inseparable. We cannot contemplate the independent action of either for an instant. If we try to do so, we find at the outset the presence of some condition or power which is due to the complementary part in our whole nature. One remarkable proof of this duality (so to speak) in our life —of all that we *are*, as far as we can observe ourselves —may be found in the fact that some speculators have seen in life nothing but the manifestation of the one element, and others nothing but the manifestation of the other, since the demonstrable presence on every occasion of either taken alone seemed to exclude the presence of the other. Nor is there, indeed, any possible refutation of the "materialist" or "spiritualist" systems except in the appeal to the individual consciousness.

6. Thus we find ourselves face to face with two great

personal problems: What is the permanent relation of soul and body? and next, What is the relation of the complex self to GOD? in which latter question is included the mystery of sin. To these may be added one other question, not personal but yet inevitable to man: What is the relation of the individual self to the world? In other words, Shall *we* be hereafter? and, if so, What shall we be? and, What is the destiny of creation generally? Round these three questions the noblest thoughts of the ancient world turned: to these the most daring speculations of later times have been addressed. What light is thrown upon them by faith in the Resurrection?

7. Our present personality, as we have seen (§ 4), involves the antithesis of soul and body. One element is not more needful to it than the other. Indeed, the clearest conception which we can form of a person is the special limitation of a self-moving power. The power must be self-moving because a person is necessarily endowed with a will which is a spring of motion. It must be limited, because, as far as our experience reaches, a will can only make itself felt in and through an organism with which it is connected. And yet, further, the mode of the limitation, including the fundamental laws by which the generic limitation is governed, the original specialities of the particular organism and the accumulated acts by which the effects of these laws and properties are modified, expresses the individual differences of personality among beings

similar in kind. This conception of personality presents to the mind an easy method of conceiving of the change of character in the same person, and likewise of the continuous effect of soul and body upon one another while the body is in constant flux. For man the body is the outward expression of the limitation in each particular case. Yet the word must be used with caution. We cannot understand by body simply a particular aggregation of matter, but an aggregation of matter as representing in one form the action of a particular law, or rather the realisation of a special formula. The specific law or formula of assimilation and combination is that which is really essential and permanent. The same material elements may enter into a thousand bodies, but the law of each body, as explained above, gives to it that which is peculiar to and characteristic of it. To take an illustration from Chemistry, the same element, pure carbon for instance, can exist in forms wholly different. This difference we represent to ourselves under the idea of some peculiar law of arrangement of the similar particles in each case. And conversely we can conceive how if the constituent element were changed the action of the different laws of arrangement (supposed to continue) would produce substances truly answering to those which resulted from their action before. Thus with regard to man, there is nothing unnatural in supposing that the power which preserves his personality by acting according to the individual law of his being in moulding the continuous changes of his present material body and all that depends upon it, will preserve his personality hereafter by still acting according to the same law in moulding the new element (so to speak) out of which a future body may be fashioned. In other words, we can understand how the law which now rules the formation of our body may find its realisation hereafter in some other element, while the new body will be essentially the same as the old one, as expressing the corresponding action of the same law in relation to the new sphere in which it may be supposed to be placed. No person is what he is solely in himself, but is in part dependent on all around him. If an individual remained unchanged while everything else changed he might be physically the same, but he would not be the same morally. There is a necessary relativity in our nature, and according to the view just indicated, since all the forms of being are changed in the new sphere of existence, each body is changed harmoniously with the remainder and in due proportion to the whole.

8. This consideration will help us in examining on grounds of simple reason the question of the permanence of our personality after death. This, as far as we can see, can happen only in two ways. It may be argued that the soul after death will itself have a personal existence; or that it will continue to act through an organisation (where the word is used in its widest sense) which is itself the expression of the same law as moulds all that we now call our body. These alternatives must be considered separately.

9. First, then, on principles of reason there seems to be no ground whatever for supposing that the soul as separate from the body is personal.[1] There is indeed an imperious instinct[2] which affirms that *we* shall survive death, but this instinct does not attempt to analyse our being, or deal with its constituent elements. It teaches simply that the dissolution of which our present senses are cognisant is not the destruction of ourselves; but it does not define, or even tend to define, in what the *I* consists, further than this. Personality implies special limitation, and this limitation (as far as we can see) is conveyed perfectly by our bodies, which, though continually changing, yet change according to one law. It is conceivable that the soul may have some individual inner limitation (so to speak), but of this we have and can have naturally no knowledge. Doubtless the soul is limited by general laws, which circumscribe its powers and capacities, for otherwise it would not only have an affinity with the infinite, but be infinite; but these general laws do not constitute individual personality. Again: if souls are originally the same at their connection with the body we cannot show how they can be so affected by it as that they should bear away, when wholly dissociated from it, the various results of the connection. Nor if they are originally different can we see how the original differ-

[1] Nothing is here said of the intermediate state of the soul after death and before the Resurrection; and probably there is something wholly deceptive in our use of words of time ("before" and "after") in such a connection. Compare Introd. § 8.

[2] Compare p. 10, n.

ences would be modified; while the assumption of the original difference introduces a fresh difficulty into the question, unless we supplement the assumption, as Plato did, by the assertion of the previous existence of souls.

10. Popular language and belief are so strong in the assertion of the personal immortality of the soul in our post-Christian times, that it is very difficult for us to realise the true state of the problem. The firmness of Christian faith, even where its presence is least suspected, influences the conclusions if not the processes of independent reasoning. Happily, the noble speculations of the Greek philosophers are a monument of what thought alone could do on this and kindred topics. Yet even here instinct will make itself felt; and again and again the sequence of an argument is broken by the independent assertion of the truth which instinct and not reason foresees or feels. One writer, however, follows the guidance of his logic to its last conclusions. In his formal treatise *On the Soul* Aristotle has examined with the most elaborate care the various elements included in it, and their mutual relations. He seems to watch the process which he guides as one wholly unconcerned in its issue. Sternly and pitilessly he states the last conclusion on man's natural hope of immortality as tested by reason; and the very coldness of his words gives them an undescribable pathos.

11. "In every natural object there are," he says,

"two elements, the one the characteristic *matter* (so to speak), which includes potentially all the manifestations of the object, and the other the causative and active principle. These differences, therefore, must exist essentially in the soul; and the rational part of man is necessarily twofold. On the one side is the 'reason' which is to be so called in virtue of its *becoming* everything; on the other that which takes its name from *making* everything, in the manner in which (to take an example) light does; for in a certain sense light makes colours existing potentially, to be colours actually. And this latter reason"—that is, the active reason which has an absolute existence—"is separable and impassive and unmixed in essence." It is not dependent in any sense on the present organism of man; it is not affected by the changes which it reveals; it is not modified in any manner by the connection in which it is placed. It is independent of a union which is begun and ended in time, "and when separated it is that alone which it is essentially." It carries with it no trace of its temporary combination with the passive "reason"; "and this alone"—this impersonal and unchangeable reason—"is immortal and eternal." It has been, and we are unconscious of the past. It will be, and we shall be unconscious of the present. "We have no recollection" of any former existence, and we shall have none hereafter of our life on earth, "because this" eternal reason, which alone survives, "is impassive, while the passive and susceptible reason"—the reason which is the seat of all personal feeling and emo-

De Animâ, iii. 5.

tion and impression—"is corruptible, and without the eternal reason is incapable of thought or consciousness."

12. One very important reflection will illustrate the force and bearing of Aristotle's judgment. We commonly interrogate the soul only as to the future: it can speak equally well of the past. Every argument for the soul's permanence hereafter, based upon its essential character, tells equally in favour of its pre-existence. Reason cannot take into account the idea of its creation; and all the presumptions drawn from what we can observe of its nature and action to show that it will be, show equally that it has been. The idea of "continuance" is equally applicable to the beginning and to the end of the life which falls under our observation. In other words, the purely logical arguments which are supposed to prove that the soul is immortal, prove that it is eternal;[1] and the legitimate deduction is, that as we

[1] In this aspect the opening chapter of the Analogy is a most instructive lesson in the weakness of pure reason to establish that hope of a future life, which has existed more or less in every period. Here only, perhaps, Bishop Butler has been unable to cast off the influences of the time in which he lived, and adopted the narrow methods of popular argument which were current in a mechanical age. Throughout he assumes that the "living being" or "agent," of which he gives no definition, is separable from our present organisation and in itself personal. And again he never notices the application of his arguments to a prior as well as to a future existence. This is the more remarkable as he considers with remarkable candour and wisdom the objection urged from the extension of his reasoning to the life of brutes. From whatever cause the defects arose, and it seems most likely that the thoughts which he failed to meet were wholly foreign to the speculations of the time, the fact remains that he assumes the two great principles

are now unconscious of any previous existence, and cannot in any way connect our present circumstances and characters in this world with our conduct in another former world, so, if we survive in any future state, we shall be equally unconscious of this through which we are now passing, and not recognise any retributive justice in the conditions under which we shall exist. At least any presumption that we shall be conscious hereafter of our present life while we are not conscious of that which we have passed through before, could only be drawn from the observation of a corresponding difference between the conditions and circumstances of our present and past lives which obviously lies wholly without the range of our faculties. For us, as far as the teaching of nature goes, this life stands absolutely alone. The application of the general experience which it gives is confined within the limits of its duration.

13. The judgment of Aristotle sums up the final result of Greek Philosophy on the soul, as a subject of pure speculation. From his time philosophy became essentially practical. The great questions of being and knowledge were merged in those of morals, in which

which above all others he ought to prove, the possibility of conceiving our personality apart from our present bodies, which, though changeable, are yet changeable according to observed laws; and next that what is true if we look back to the first origin of our present life is not true if we look forward to its close. How momentous the latter assumption is may be seen at once if any one will substitute "birth" for "death" and "origin" for "destruction" in the earlier arguments of the chapter. The former assumption is even more obviously the assumption of the chief point in the conclusion.

intuition has a legitimate exercise. Later writers, therefore, furnish nothing of importance to the exact discussion of the hope of immortality; but it is impossible not to compare the conclusions of Aristotle with those of Plato. The master is as confident and sanguine as the scholar is sceptical and passionless. But the method of Plato is as full of instruction as the results of Aristotle. Plato is sure of his belief beforehand. His arguments are merely to justify it. And when he feels that these—though strengthened by the bold proposition that we *do* bring with us to earth traces of our former existence—are unequal to support the weight of his conclusion, he makes, as he expresses it, a bold venture, and presents the substance of his faith in one of those magnificent myths, by which he endeavours to bridge over the chasm between the seen and unseen worlds.[1] His "Republic" closes with the noble legend of Er the son of Armenius, who saw in a trance the judgment of the dead, and the hidden glories of the world. For once, he tells us, a soul was allowed to return to the body without drinking the waters of Forgetfulness. And so "this story was saved and not lost, and it will save us," he adds, "should we listen to its teaching; and then we shall happily cross the river of Lethe and not defile our souls; but deeming that the soul is immortal and capable of bearing every evil and winning every good, we shall keep close to the upward path, and practise in every way justice and wisdom, that we may be friends

Plat. *Resp.* x. 621.

[1] I venture to refer for a fuller discussion of these myths to the *Contemporary Review*, 1866.

to ourselves and friends to the gods." "To confidently affirm that [the fate of souls] is such as I have described," Socrates says at the end of the *Phaedo*, "becomes no reasonable man. But I do think that it becomes him to believe that it is either this or like this, if at least the soul is shown to be immortal; and that it is worthy of him to face peril boldly in such a belief, for the peril is glorious; and such thoughts he ought to use as a charm to allay his own misgivings, in which spirit I have myself dwelt thus long upon the story." For in such questions the really brave man "will either learn or discover the truth, or if this be impossible he will take at any rate the best of human words and that which is most irrefragable, and carried on this as on a raft sail through life in perpetual jeopardy, unless one might make the journey on a securer vessel, some divine word if it might be, more surely and with less peril."

Plat. *Phaedo*, 114.

Plat. *Phaedo*, 85.

14. If then pure reason cannot suggest any arguments to establish the personality of the soul when finally separated from the body, and for *us* personality is only another name for existence, still less can it show any grounds for supposing that it possesses in itself the power of assuming at death another organisation corresponding to our present body whereby its personality may be preserved. Our present body is not in any way, as far as we can see, due primarily to the action of the soul, which acts through and upon it; and when the body is dissolved, the only action of the soul of which

we can have naturally any knowledge ceases. It may have some inherent energy in virtue of which it manifests itself throughout the ages, now in this form, now in that. It may, but that seems harder to conceive, have gained on earth the means of realising a personal existence hereafter. It may, as many thought even among GOD'S ancient people, go back to Him who gave it and continue to exist only as part of His Infinite Being. Our utter incapacity of forming a clear conception of any mode of existence differing in essence from our own, and not simply in extent of similar powers, forces us to contemplate these and other alternatives, and to withhold our judgment till we gain some new light. If we look within or without we have absolutely no analogy to carry our thoughts one step onward into a realm wholly unknown: none to show that the soul will exert a power there which has been undeveloped or dormant here. Every change which we can follow is simply of the earth. Faith, or love, or instinct, may cross the dark river, but they go alone: reason cannot follow them. Nay more: reason shows that the visions which they see are mere shadowy projections of what we see and feel now.

15. Thus we are placed before a final contradiction. On the one side we are so constituted as to cling to the belief in the continuance of our personality after death: on the other reason points to death as a phenomenon absolutely singular which closes life, as far as we know it, and takes away the conditions of our life. But if a single experience can show that these conditions are not destroyed, but suspended as far as we observe them, or modified by the action of some new law: that what seems to be a dissolution is really a transformation: that the soul does not remain alone in a future state, but is still united with our body, that is with an organism which in a new sphere expresses the law which our present body now expresses in this (*supra*, § 7); then reason will welcome the belief in our future personality no less than instinct. For the truth is not against reason but beyond it. Reason shows simply that what we commonly see, and what we can learn from the analysis of our own nature, lends no support to the conclusion which we cannot abandon. But let some new fact come in, and all will be changed, if that reveals to us something of the character of life after death.

16. Such a fact is the Resurrection. In one sense no event can be more natural than this, so far as it answers to a craving for knowledge of the unseen world, which by its intensity indicates that it was intended to be satisfied, as much as any other original instinct of man. In another sense nothing can be more beyond nature, for it introduces us to a novel phase of being, of which we feel even in the presence of this revelation that we can know only a part darkly and "in a riddle." For the Resurrection is not like any one of the recorded miracles of raising from the dead. It is not a restoration to the old life, to its wants, to its special limitations, to its inevitable close, but the revelation of a new life

foreshadowing new powers of action and a new mode of being. It issues not in death but in the Ascension, for which it is the preparation and the condition. It is not an extension of an existence with which we are acquainted, but the manifestation of an existence for which we hope. It is not like any of the fabled apotheoses of the friends of gods, whose spirits, purified by the funeral fire from the stains of earth, were carried to the immediate presence of those whom they had loved, but it is the consecration of a restored and perfected manhood. It is not a withdrawal from men or a laying aside of humanity, complete, final, and immediate, but the pledge of an abiding communion of a Saviour with the fulness of our nature on earth and in heaven. It is not the putting off of the body, but the transfiguration of it. And so in its record it is not like any of the dreams in which earlier poets had endeavoured to convey to others the hope which they cherished. Its teaching is conveyed in a series of facts. Now one incident and now another brings out some aspect of the whole truth, as far as we can apprehend it. But all incidents alike are simple and in a certain sense natural. No vision is opened of glory or suffering. No display is made of fresh powers. No overpowering exhibition of majesty strikes unwilling conviction into the hearts of those who were before unbelieving.[1] The Lord rose

John xx. 17.

[1] It has been objected that our Lord revealed Himself only to believers or to those inclined to believe. If we regard the Resurrection as a revelation of a *new* life it is obvious that it could not have been otherwise. In order to establish the belief in the reality of this new existence it was necessary that some power should exist in the witnesses

from the grave; and those who had known Him before, knew that He was the same and yet changed. This is the sum of the Apostle's testimony, the new Gospel of the world.

17. In this connection there is one most important consideration which is commonly overlooked. The Apostles announce the fact of the Resurrection and its immediate bearing upon the individual hopes of men, but they do not develop its significance. The fact is added to the sum of human experience. The interpretation of it is left for life. And so it is that with the comments of eighteen centuries its meaning is yet unexhausted. Deeper insight, wider sympathies, grander

to apprehend it. There was a spiritual side to the manifestation of the Risen Christ which could only be discerned spiritually. If it had been necessary merely to show the restoration of the Lord to the condition of an ordinary human life, as in the case of Lazarus, the testimony of indifferent spectators would have been adequate. But if the appearances were designed to be a revelation of a glorified human life, then the manifestation to unbelievers would not only have been contrary to the usual method of the Providence of God, but also, as far as we can see, unavailing. For if the Lord had appeared to them as a man simply, their evidence would have gone to establish a false view of His Risen Person: if He had appeared to them under new conditions of being, they would have been unable to acknowledge the reality of His manifestation. The believer who had familiarly known Christ and felt His power could alone grasp and harmonise the two modes of the Revelation of His Person. Afterwards, when the idea of the Risen Christ was fully established, we find an appearance granted to St. Paul, which carried with it immediate conviction to an unbeliever; but till this idea was established, as far as we can judge, such an appearance would have been without effect. The appearance to St. Paul was as real as the others (ὤφθη) but made under different circumstances. It was a revelation of Christ glorified, and as such left its impression on all the teaching of St. Paul.

aspirations, have been granted to men in the progress of ages, but the idea of the Resurrection penetrates beneath and beyond all the thoughts which history or science has hitherto made known. The Gospel is still the same, but known more fully with ever-growing clearness as the successive crises of thought and life have shown its fitness for meeting them. And it is obvious why this is so. The Resurrection is a new creation. Its issues cannot be contemplated by man at first, though its utmost consequences are included in its actual realisation. And just as in the creative works of human genius harmonies and lessons are found in virtue of their relation to absolute truth, of which their authors were never conscious, so in this which *is* the Truth, all later speculation will find fresh light upon the problems of human existence.

18. There are indeed passages, especially in the Epistle to the Ephesians and in the writings of St. John, in which the Apostles announce mysteries springing out of the Resurrection which are only now dawning upon the students of history and life; but as a general rule they declare the fact that "Christ rose again" without dwelling on those aspects of its meaning for which men were not at that time prepared by knowledge or experience. In this respect the narratives of the Resurrection are unparalleled. The Evangelists[1] record

[1] At this point I shall use the writings of the New Testament without reserve. If the Resurrection is admitted on other grounds to be a fact, no one will (I believe) question the general veracity of the Evangelists.

the miracle so calmly, looking solely, as we must think, at its historic aspect, that in reading of it we lose sight of its stupendous significance from the natural simplicity of the details in which its lessons are conveyed. The manifestations of the risen Saviour are mixed with scenes of fear, of misgiving, of unbelief. He appeared in Galilee and at Jerusalem: now at night and again in the early morning: in the upper room and under the open sky: in an assembly gathered, as it would seem, for religious exercise, and to men busy with their ordinary work. Nothing is (if we may so speak) farther from the thought of the Evangelists than to give a doctrinal view of the mystery which they declare. Christ was the same and yet changed. That was in substance what they had to tell; and in that lies the full answer to the first great question before us. The body is not destroyed by death. Its union with the soul is for a time (as we are forced to conceive of it, though perhaps quite wrongly) interrupted but not closed. Our speculative doubts are met, as they could only be met, by a fact.

19. It is unnecessary to dwell on the various details by which the identity of the Lord's human body is brought out in the Gospels. It is obvious from a mere enumeration that they meet each misgiving. The body which the disciples had laid in the sepulchre was no longer to be found when they looked for it. The marks of the Passion were made sensibly present in the Risen Saviour to him who would not

John xx.

otherwise believe. Nay more, Christ Himself offered this very proof to those who "supposed that they had seen a spirit." "Behold my hands and my feet, that it is I myself: handle me, and see, for a spirit hath not flesh and bones, as ye see me have." . . . "And He took [meat] and did eat before them." And it can hardly be without reference to this incident that St. John in his Epistle reckons this "handling" last among the various revelations which GOD had given of His Son. The length of time too during which the appearances were extended familiarised the disciples (so to speak) with the mystery which had at first filled them with terror. For forty days He "showed Himself alive to them by many infallible proofs, being seen of them and speaking of the things pertaining to the kingdom of God."

Luke xxiv. 39, 43.

Compare John xx. 20. Compare John xxi.

1 John i. 1.

Acts i. 3.

20. But this Body which was recognised as essentially the same Body, had yet undergone some marvellous change, of which we can gain a faint idea by what is directly recorded of its manifestations.[1] Thus we find that the Person of Christ was not recognised directly by those who saw Him. However firm their conviction

[1] It is not, I believe, a mere fancy to see a typical indication of this change in the words used by our Lord Himself of His glorified Body: Luke xxiv. 39 ("flesh and bones"). The significant variation from the common formula "flesh and blood" must have been at once intelligible to Jews, accustomed to the provisions of the Mosaic ritual, and nothing would have impressed upon them more forcibly the transfiguration of Christ's Body than the verbal omission of the element of blood which was for them the symbol and seat of corruptible life.

was afterwards that they had "seen the Lord," they knew Him first when He was pleased to make Himself known. Human sense alone was not capable of discerning Who He was. It could not be otherwise if His Body was glorified, for our senses can only apprehend that which is of kindred nature with themselves. At one time it was by a word of general or personal tenderness that Christ awakened the faith by which sense was quickened: at another time by the celebration of that holy rite which He had instituted before His death: at another by a mighty act which symbolised the blessing of the Apostolic work.

Matt. xxviii. 9. John xx. 16, 19.

Luke xxiv. 30, 31. John xxi.

21. And as Christ's Body was no longer necessarily to be recognised, so also it was not bound by the material laws to which its action was generally conformed. He is found present, no one knows from whence. He passes away, no one knows whither. He stands in the midst of the little group of the Apostles "when the doors were shut for fear of the Jews." "He vanished out of the sight" of those whose eyes were opened that they knew Him. And at last "while they beheld, He was taken up, and a cloud received Him out of their sight." It is impossible not to feel in reading the narratives that we are regarding a form of existence human, indeed, yet indefinitely ennobled by the removal of needs and limitations to which we are at present subject. It is vain for us to speculate on the nature of

John xx. 19, 26. Luke xxiv. 31.

Acts i. 9.

that transformed human Body. We can form no clear positive conception which is not shaped by the present laws of thought. Negatively we can only say that it was not bound by those laws of space (for example) which necessarily enter into all that we think or do. The life which is revealed to us is not the continuation of the present life, but a life which takes up into itself all the elements of our present life, and transfigures them by a glorious change, which we can regard at present only under signs and figures.

22. Thus the Resurrection answers as completely as it can be answered the first great question by which we are met. In the Person of Christ we see the whole of man, his body and soul, raised together from the grave. No part is left behind. The whole complex nature is raised and glorified. It is not that the soul only lives; nor yet that the body, such as it was before, is restored to its former vigour. The Saviour, as far as we regard His Manhood, is not unclothed, to use St. Paul's image, but clothed upon. Nothing is taken away, but something is added by which all that was before present is transfigured. "The corruptible puts on incorruption: the mortal puts on immortality."

2 Cor. v. 4.

1 Cor. xv. 54.

23. This thought brings us to the second question, the final relation of man to God, of man, that is, as subject to the consequences of sin. And here it will

be necessary to consider somewhat carefully the idea which lies at the root of sin, lest it may seem that we are dealing with a mere phantom. But still we may leave out of our investigation some questions which have been connected with it. Our inquiry does not extend to the obstacles which material nature places in the way of man, of whatever form they may be, nor yet to the mutual relations of animals to one another or to man. We are obviously wholly incapable of knowing anything of the position in which any beings except ourselves stand towards GOD, or of their latent powers, or of their future destiny. It is quite conceivable that what appears to us in the light of suffering and decay in beings wholly unlike ourselves may to a higher intelligence assume a different aspect; or (and this seems even from a view of nature far more probable) the fate of the physical and animal creation may be bound up by some mysterious influence with that of man. At least, we can see the difference between what we call evil in inorganic or brute nature, and evil (moral evil) in man which involves the operation of a free will, and an acknowledged relation between the person of the sinner and GOD. Whether these conditions of action can exist in the case of other creatures or not we are wholly unable to determine; but it is at least remarkable that as soon as the phenomena of free will are observable in animals (as in the case of those which have been long associated with man) we attribute to them a measure of responsibility by according praise and blame to their actions.

24. If then we look at the problem in its simplest form it is evident that the possibility of sin is necessarily included in the creation of a finite, free being; for the simplest idea which we can form of sin is the finite setting itself up against the infinite. Selfishness, which exists potentially as soon as "self" exists, is the ground of all sin. Hence we can see how a perfect finite being may yet be exposed to temptation, for the sense of limitation brings with it the thought, or the possibility of the thought, of passing the limit.

25. And not only is a perfect finite being in this way necessarily under a moral probation, but the actual existence of sin is not required for his moral development. It is necessary to dwell on this point, for if it could be shown that sin belongs essentially to the idea of individual human progress as one of the conditions of its realisation, we might at once dismiss as vain the obstinate questionings with which we ponder over its future issues. It is only if sin is an intrusive corruption of our nature that we need feel anxious about the permanence of its results. But it follows from the final analysis of sin which has been given that man, though he had not sinned, might yet have practised some (at least) essentially human virtues: all indeed which are comprised in self-control and the recognition of dependence. Nothing, therefore, can be more false than to say that "moral good and moral evil—as distinguished from the *possibility* of good and evil—came into being together." A command implies the possibility of obedience

and disobedience, but obedience is no less real though disobedience in fact never takes place. Love, again, the centre of all social virtues, and truth the centre of all intellectual virtues, are both wholly independent of the presence of evil among men.

26. But it may be said that if moral evil were removed from the world "life would be impoverished." So indeed it appears at first sight to us who are habituated to the startling contrasts of life : for us shadow is a necessity of distinct vision. Yet it would be difficult to show that the more splendid qualities which are brought out (for instance) by war are better, in any sense, than their correlatives which need no such field for their display : that the heroic forgetfulness or contempt of danger or suffering, which springs from a great passion or a generous impulse in the midst of a fierce conflict or under the sense of a deep wrong, is better than that rational self-control which we have seen can exist in the highest degree without the presence of evil. We are too apt to think that virtue which is seen on a larger scale is itself magnified. On the other hand it may be allowed that evil itself serves as part of our discipline : that it gives occasion for the exercise of special virtues, and by antagonism calls them into play ; yet this is only to say that it has been so ordered that evil shall in some degree minister to its own defeat.

27. And while we grant that in society evil may be the occasion of good, it is by no means clear that this is

true in the individual. As far as we can see, the presence of evil, that is, the wilful transgression of limit as distinguished from the original limitation, is neither the occasion nor the condition of good, nor on the narrow stage of human life the preliminary to it. The highest conception of active virtue—duty—is absolutely untouched by it both in its origin and in its fulfilment, even when evil is regarded under the extreme form of pain.

28. Moreover it must be observed that evil, while it may be the occasion of good, is never transmuted into good. Evil remains evil to the last in whatever form it may show itself. Sin remains sin: pain remains pain: ignorance (so far as it is culpable) remains ignorance: though sin and pain and ignorance may call forth efforts of love and fortitude and patience.

29. Nor can it be said that sin realised, and not merely the possibility of sin by the action of a free will, is the necessary condition of human virtue, and consequently of human happiness. For if this were true, then it would follow either that evil itself will be eternal, or that human life in its true sense will cease to be. Whatever may be the function of evil in the social discipline of men whose powers are already impaired by sin, we have no reason to think that evil could find any place for giving occasion to new or higher good in a society of men animated by those active and personal virtues which have been seen to be wholly independent of it (§§ 25, 27); not to speak

of the possibility of other forms of virtuous character inconceivable in our present mixed state; for the permanence of the antitypes or perfections of our present virtues in another state by no means excludes the possibility of the existence of other virtues as yet unknown, which may come into play from the manifestations of new relations between ourselves or of ourselves to other intelligent beings.

30. It follows then that sin—moral evil as involving the action of will—is in fact something wholly foreign to human nature: that in its essential character it remains always evil even when it is the occasion of good: that it is not a lower form of goodness or a necessary condition for its exercise, but the conscious transgression of limit: that in the individual it leads to no good: that even in society at large its disciplinary power only effects by sacrifice and imperfectly what the observance of the true bounds of nature would effect perfectly. It is then a foreign element in our nature, and absolutely abhorrent from our proper destiny. But it is also, as far as reason can trace, permanent in its issues. If therefore a belief in personal immortality be held on any grounds except those furnished by the Gospel, it must be accompanied by an awful sense of the consequences of past offences.

31. It is this fact which gives to the idea of sin its most terrible significance. As far as we can conceive by the help of reason the effects of every action must

be infinite, and in regard to the agent (whatever they may be to others) corresponding to and like the action. But all sin (as such) necessarily involves the idea of suffering to the person who commits it; for selfishness, the final element of sin, is the contrary of love, and therefore when set against Infinite Love must bring the misery of unavailing desire and isolation. Hence punishment (for all consequences must at last be referred to the Will of the Personal Creator), or (in another light) suffering as the natural consequence of selfishness, must exist as long as sin exists; and so in any particular case the past sin must still work its full effect in separating the sinner from God without end, unless some new power be interposed.

32. For it must be noticed that suffering has in itself no power or tendency to remove or expiate sin, the consequences of which are best conceived as evolved (so to speak) naturally and centring in the changed character of the guilty, and not imposed externally according to any fixed standard. Nor again has it in itself any power to produce repentance, by which in the intercourse of man and man the effects of wrong-doing, as far as their mutual relations are concerned, may be removed. But even in this latter case no repentance can cancel the consequences of the wrong action, either without the doer or within him. These throughout life and (as far as we can see) beyond it are inwrought into the world and into his nature. Future punishment is a conclusion of reason, if we grant the

future continuance of our personality. The mystery which reason cannot of itself apprehend is that this punishment can be stayed. Thus if we approach the subject from this side it is the forgiveness, or rather the "washing away" of sins, and not their punishment, which is the real subject of Revelation. If, on the other hand, we confine our view to this life, the idea of a Supreme Being tempering suffering with a view to repentance answers to an instinct of man and not to any logical process; and Scripture first teaches us to believe that the instinct is true.

33. For just as there is an instinct within us which claims the inheritance of a future life, so we feel that after sin repentance is still possible and efficacious, and that our Heavenly Father can do away our sins. But Reason which deserted us before equally deserts us now. It tells us from the observation of what we see around and from the conception which we are forced to make of the dependence of the future on the past, that we must be for ever, in relation to GOD, what we are, and bear about with us the scars and wounds which sin has inflicted upon us.

34. Here, again, the fact of the Resurrection meets our doubts with a new Revelation. If we look at our Lord simply as He was seen outwardly, He bore in Himself all the consequences of sin. "He was tempted in all points like as we are" except by personal sin. He took our flesh, with its

Heb. iv. 15.

liabilities to hunger, and fatigue, and pain, upon Him: He shared the emotions of anger, and sorrow, and affection: He bore death with its most terrible accompaniments, the last issue of sin, and that sense of utter isolation from God which is its complete punishment. Whatever sin could work He took upon Himself, and when all was ended God raised Him up "for our justification," and the Lord Jesus bore our human nature, over which sin had no longer power, to the immediate presence of the Father.

Matt. xxvii. 46.

35. But it will be said that the Lord's sufferings were not the result (as ours are) of personal sin, and consequently that we can draw no comfort from His triumph over death. To this objection it is in part an answer to reply that the sufferings of Christ were as though they were due to Himself, and that not by a fiction, but by His real assumption of human nature. How this could be in regard to the more general consequences of sin, as want or grief, is sufficiently intelligible from the fact that He was truly man. But how He could take sin upon Him is a mystery which we cannot solve, though in fact it is only a mystery of the same kind as His "becoming flesh" (compare § 38). Yet even here so much at least we can see, that in the Agony and on the Cross He suffered, yet with an intensity which we cannot appreciate, even as those do who bear the consequences of personal sin. "He offered up prayers and supplications with strong crying and tears unto Him that was

John i. 14.

Heb. v. 7.

able to save Him from death, and was heard in that He feared."

36. The complete answer lies somewhat deeper, as has been already indicated, in the recognition of our Lord's Divine Person. It is impossible to understand the Resurrection completely apart from the Incarnation. It may indeed he said that the Resurrection is the historic seal of the Incarnation, which remains for ever a mystery removed from all witness. And it was in this sense that the first teachers of Christianity understood and interpreted it. After the Resurrection, as we have seen (i. §§ 56 ff.), they saw in Christ a Saviour of boundless power. His Life and Death were contemplated in their atoning virtue: His Name was given as that whereby men might be saved: in Him was Life. The contrast between that which was apprehended, if with the deepest reverence we may so speak, as personal discipline and redeeming power, was placed in its broadest light. "It became" GOD "to make Him perfect through suffering," and even thus "He tasted death for every man." He was "declared to be the Son of GOD with power, according to the Spirit of holiness, by the resurrection from the dead." And "though He were a Son, yet learned He obedience by the things which He suffered; and being made perfect, He became the author of eternal salvation unto all them that obey Him."

Heb. ii. 9, 10.

Rom. i. 4.

Heb. v. 8, 9.

37. Apart from this faith in the Divinity of Christ,

His Resurrection loses its highest significance. It has in itself and absolutely no direct and immediate connection with ourselves. It is an isolated incident in the history of mankind, glorious and full of hope but not the new birth of humanity. It answers to that view of the Lord which represents Him as a Teacher simply, and does not, according to the Apostolic pattern, bring out into chief prominence what He did and what He was. If Christ was only man, such as we are in nature, then His triumph over death is no Gospel for those who are bowed down with the weight of guilt. In Him we can feel that "the Prince of this world when He came had nothing": Death could not hold Him. For ourselves, we "receive" in corruption "the due reward of our deeds: but this man hath done nothing amiss."

John xiv. 30.

Luke xxiii. 41.

38. On such a theory no hope like that of St. Paul could repose. But once introduce the belief in Christ's Divine nature, and His Death and Resurrection are no longer of the individual but of the race. Nor in doing this are we taking refuge in an arbitrary assumption to help our argument. On the contrary, we simply repeat the interpretation which the Apostles placed on the whole work of the Saviour. It was on this belief that the Church was founded and built up. The belief was not indeed always drawn out with exact precision, yet it was always implied in the relation which the believer was supposed to hold to God in Christ. The formula of Baptism, which has never changed, is unin-

telligible without it. The Eucharist is emptied of the blessing which every age has sought in that Holy Sacrament, if it be taken away.

39. If Christ took our nature upon Him (as we believe) by an act of love, it was not that of one but of all. He was not one man only among men, but in Him all humanity was gathered up. And thus now as at all time mankind are (so to speak) organically united with Him. His acts are in a true sense our acts, so far as we realise the union: His death is our death: His Resurrection, our Resurrection. Nothing can be plainer than the assertion of this doctrine. Our "bodies are members of Christ"; and conversely a Christian society is "a body of Christ." "I have been," St. Paul says, "crucified with Christ." If we died "with Christ," he writes to the Romans, "we believe that we shall also live with Him. . . . Reckon ye also yourselves to be dead indeed unto sin, but living unto God *in* Christ Jesus." And yet more plainly, "When we were dead in sins [God] quickened us together with Christ, and raised us up together, and made us sit together in the heavenly realm in Christ Jesus." "In whom also ye were circumcised with the circumcision made without hands, in putting off the body of the sins of the flesh, in the circumcision of Christ; buried with Him in baptism, wherein also ye were raised with Him through faith in the operation of

1 Cor. vi. 15.

1 Cor. xii. 27.

Gal. ii. 20.

Eph. ii. 5, 6.

Col. ii. 11, 12.

God, who raised Him from the dead." So again St. Peter speaks of God "who begat us again to a living hope through the resurrection of Jesus Christ from the dead"; and his final salutation is "Peace be with you all who are *in* Christ Jesus."

1 Pet. i. 3.

1 Pet. v. 14.

40. The ground of these and similar statements is found in the words of our Lord, which first receive through them their full significance. "Abide in me and I in you. . . . I am the Vine; ye are the branches. He that abideth in Me and I in him, the same bringeth forth much fruit; for apart from Me ye can do nothing." And again, in His last great prayer for His disciples, He says: "For their sakes I sanctify Myself, that they also may be sanctified in truth. Neither pray I for these alone, but for them also which believe on Me through their word, that they all may be one; as Thou, Father, art in Me, and I in Thee, that they also may be in Us. . . I in them, and Thou in Me, that they may be made perfect into one."

John xv. 4, 5.

John xvii. 19-23.

41. The full doctrine of the Resurrection cannot be understood without constant reference to these deeper revelations of Christ's Person; nor, again, is the Apostolic doctrine of the Person of Christ intelligible without the light of the glorious manifestations of Himself which He made to His disciples after He was risen from the dead. But it is not our object now to follow out the mutual

relations of these two elements of our Creed, or to trace them both back to the Incarnation. It is enough to have indicated in what way we can conceive that the efficacy of the Resurrection is extended to those for whom Christ died; and having done this we may next notice how the teaching of the Resurrection on the dignity of the body tends to explain the relation of the individual self to the world.

42. The noblest of the ancient moralists looked upon man's body as a hopeless burden and fatal hindrance to the soul; and in this they have been followed by the noblest non-Christian moralists in every age. The famous thanksgiving of Plotinus that "he was not tied to an immortal body" expresses the common feeling of all who have not felt the power of the Resurrection. But Christianity transfigures what philosophy would destroy. It shows that the corruption by which we are weighed down does not belong to our proper nature, and is not necessarily bound up with it for ever. It lays open with a deeper and more searching criticism than a system of morality could direct, the internal struggles to which the "flesh" must give occasion, and the inevitable defeats which we must suffer in our efforts towards the divine life. Plato does not describe more sadly than St. Paul the afflictions by which we are beset while yet oppressed by "the body of humiliation." Or to take an example from a different sect and age, M. Aurelius does not express more keenly than St. John a sense of the evils of the

Phil. iii. 21.

present life. But there is an immeasurable chasm between the Apostles and Platonists or Stoics. "We that are in this tabernacle do groan, being burdened," St. Paul writes: "not for that we would be unclothed, but clothed upon, that mortality may be swallowed up by life." The better change for which he longed was not the destruction but the ennobling of his body, so that it might "be fashioned like unto [Christ's] body of glory, according to the working whereby He is able even to subdue all things unto Himself." And the power by which this transformation should be effected was the simple contemplation of Christ in His essential majesty. Nay, in some sense the change is already begun on earth, so far as that we can look forward with full hope to its accomplishment; for "we all, with open face beholding as in a glass the glory of the Lord, are changed into the same image from glory to glory." "Beloved, now are we the sons of God," such are St. John's words, "and it doth not yet appear what we shall be: but we know that, when He shall appear, we shall be like him, *for we shall see Him as He is.*"

2 Cor. v. 4.

Phil. iii. 21.

2 Cor. iii. 18.

1 John iii. 2.

43. In a word, our present body is as the seed of our future body. The one rises as naturally from the other as the flower from the germ. "It is sown in corruption, it is raised in incorruption: it is sown in dishonour, it is raised in glory: it is sown in weakness, it is raised in power: it is sown a natural

1 Cor. xv.

body, it is raised a spiritual body." We cannot, indeed, form any conception of the change which shall take place, except so far as it is shown to us in the Person of the Lord. Its fulfilment is in another state, and our thoughts are bound by this state. But there is nothing against reason in the analogy. Every change of life which we can observe now must be from one material form to another equally falling under our senses; but such a change may help us to understand how a form at present sensible may pass through a great crisis into another, which is an expression of the same law of life, though our present senses cannot naturally take cognisance of it (*supra*, § 7). If the analogy were to explain the passage of man from an existence of one kind (limited by a body) to an existence of another kind (unlimited by a body), it would then be false; but as it is, it illustrates by a vivid figure the perpetuity of our bodily life, as proved in the Resurrection of Christ.

44. The moral significance of such a doctrine as the Resurrection of the body cannot be over-rated. Both personally and socially it places the sanctions if not the foundations of morality on a new ground. Each sin against the body is no longer a stain on that which is itself doomed to perish, but a defilement of that which is consecrated to an eternal life. To injure another, is to injure one with whom we are bound by the closest ties through a common fellowship in Christ. "The body is not for fornication, but for

1 Cor. vi. 13-15.

the Lord; and the Lord for the body. And God both raised up the Lord, and will also raise up us by His power. Know you not that your bodies are the members of Christ?" "Speak every man truth with his neighbour: for we are members one of another." Each Christian society is "a body of Christ," of which the members are charged with various functions; and these "bodies" again are "members" of other "bodies" wider and greater, and these at last "members" of that universal Church which is the "fulness of Christ," its heavenly Head.

Eph. iv. 25.

45. In this way the doctrine of the Resurrection turned into a reality the exquisite myth of Plato, in which he represented tyrants and great men waiting for their final sentence from the judges of Hades, with their bodies scarred and wounded by lust and passion and cruelty. And at the same time the notion of civic union, in which lay so much of the strength and virtue of classical life, is freed from the dangers of party and class and extended to the utmost limits of a human brotherhood. The earliest religious instinct of men taught them to regard each class, each guild, each city, each state, as standing in a corporate connection with some particular deity, and enjoying his protection: Christianity satisfies the instinct, and harmonises the idea of a special relationship to a Divine Lord with that of catholic union in Him. It gives the largest range to the sympathies and obligations of men at the very time when it lays the greatest weight on

Plat. *Gorg.* 524 f.

the distinct importance and eternal issues of every isolated human action.

46. The perfect reconciliation of the claims and duties of the individual and of the society is no less characteristic of the teaching of Christianity than the hallowing (so to speak) of the mutual relationship of soul and body; and both doctrines alike find their historical basis and the pledge of their realisation in the Resurrection. In præ-Christian times the individual was either sacrificed to the state or contemplated wholly apart from it. The Platonist, in theory, regarded the man in a perfect society as simply living for it, and having independently no personal worth. The Stoic stood apart in proud loneliness, and looked on the turmoil of statesmanship and war with the stern indifference of despair or resignation. In practice both were more or less unfaithful to their creed. Socrates found problems of life which were so absorbing that till he had solved these, he affirmed that he could not interfere with politics. M. Aurelius, while he steeled himself against the future by steadfastly affirming the existence of a fatal cycle of human destinies, yet laboured with a faithful will to discharge the offices of the empire. But neither had any principle to justify the combination of the conflicting elements of action and thought. Nature only was stronger than logic. But the Apostles could declare that the sanctity of the man rests on the same fact as the sanctity of the society; that the dignity of personal action is not in conflict, but in absolute harmony, with that of social

action: that duties to self and to others are simply different expressions of the same belief in one absolute unity. No power which has ever effectually stirred men to heroism or self-devotion is lost, but all are seen in one source.

47. The glorious view which is thus opened of the one life "fulfilled in many ways" which animates mankind, potentially at least, does not exhaust the prospect which Christianity offers to the eye of faith. Glimpses are given of a yet wider harmony and a vaster change. Reference has been made already to the passages in which the Apostolic writings notice the fellowship of nature in the blessings of Redemption (i. § 1). It is evident from our ignorance of the forces at work in the outer world, of which we can observe only some effects according to our limited powers of perception, that we are quite unable to form any notion of "a new heaven and a new earth." Yet the fact of the Resurrection of the body suggests more forcibly the literal truth of that "restitution of all things" which was announced from the first by St. Peter. The ennobling of our material organisation contains, as it were, the promise of a more complete transfiguration of Nature. It is possible that the change lies nearer to us than we are apt to imagine. It may perhaps be the case that what appear to us to be imperfections and evils in the physical or animal world may derive the character which we attribute to them from the incompleteness of our own faculties; and that

Acts iii. 21.

this transfiguration (relative to us) may lie within us and not without (compare § 23).[1]

48. Whether this view is true or not, it contains an important element of truth which is commonly neglected. What we call "laws of nature" are, as has been seen (Introd. § 8), nothing more than laws of our present observation of nature. They are a resultant, so to speak, of some unknown force without and our own powers of sensation and thought. The permanence of the law depends on the permanence of these two elements: if either is changed the resultant is also changed. If then our bodily powers are transfigured, as we see in the Resurrection of the Lord, our powers of observation and the limitations (as of space or time and the like) according to which we class phenomena, will undergo a proportionate change. Thus for us the "law" will be changed while the power whose working we notice and describe by it is itself unchanged. But still there is no abruptness, no arbitrary revolution, in this new aspect of Nature. The new law must be conceived as springing out of our new powers, just as the present law springs from our present powers, when they are turned to the objects which fall under them. If our present body is the germ of that which will be, so is the present law of that which will hereafter regulate our perceptions. Thus to the Christian the laws of Nature are not laws

[1] This thought, I now find, has been admirably worked out by Mr. Hinton, whose *Life and Letters* is full of illustrations of the argument which I have suggested.

only, but prophecies. In the light of the Resurrection they are symbols of something broader and more glorious beyond them. They do not confine hope but guide it.

49. The line of thought which has been just opened leads to the Christian solution—as far as a solution is possible—of the last question which arises out of the simplest views of life, our relation to the world; but the fuller discussion of this must be reserved for a separate section. Meanwhile we have gained some insight into the doctrinal significance of the Resurrection in relation to the fulness of our future personal existence and to our hope of restoration before God. It has been seen that our present self is essentially twofold; and that we cannot in any way conceive that we can remain the same if either of the elements of which it is made up wants its proper representative. The doctrine of the "immortality of the soul" is therefore wholly insufficient to satisfy that desire for a life hereafter for which man naturally craves. In confirmation of this conclusion it has been shown that Aristotle and Plato, while regarding the subject from very different points of view, equally indicate that no arguments of pure reason can establish the future personal existence of the soul, as a conscious continuance of our present existence. Aristotle denies the conclusion on the strength of a direct analysis: Plato clothes his instinctive hope in the form of a story; confessing, as it were, that his logical process fails him. Yet further, the arguments which point forward, point backward also, and thus fail to establish

the conscious dependence of the future on the present. Introduce the belief in the Resurrection and each difficulty disappears. In the Person of the Lord we see how we can hereafter be the same and yet indefinitely ennobled: how our souls and bodies may be for ever united, so that the individual self remains, while the body is transformed by a glorious change.

50. In the next place it has been shown that while the possibility of sin is necessarily included in the existence of a free finite will, actual sin is wholly alien from the perfection of man's nature: that in itself and in the individual sin is inherently and immutably bad, though it may give occasion to good by antagonism; and that while it is such it must bring with it suffering which has no virtue to remove sin or the consequences of sin, of which it is itself one. In the way of nature then we cannot see how the evil of which we are conscious can ever cease to work out torment, though at the same time we instinctively turn to God as a Father ready to forgive and also (but how we know not) wash away sin. Again in this aspect the Resurrection presents to us the fulfilment of man's triumph in Christ over the issues of sin, which culminate in death. But here the full significance of the Resurrection, and our personal share in it, is seen to be bound up with the Apostolic teaching on the Person of Christ as unfolded in His Life and Ascension, on which the Church was founded, and in which we find all our hopes fulfilled, in virtue of a fellowship potential for the race and actual

by faith for the individual. "In Christ" we can stand without fear in the very presence of God.

51. Further, we have been led to notice some of the moral consequences of a belief in the Resurrection: how it reveals a majesty in the body which philosophers have denied, and the consequent importance of every human action: how it hallows with a new sanction the idea of society at the same time and in the same way as it raises the dignity of the individual: how it harmonises, by the faith in the gathering together of all humanity in Christ, claims which before were thought to be contradictory in their origin and in their fulfilment: how finally it casts a light over the destiny of the world and helps us to understand how our perception of nature will be indefinitely raised, even if nature itself is unchanged, by the ennobling of our own faculties, and the removal or proportionate transformation of those limitations by which they are at present confined.

It remains to consider more in detail some of these thoughts as illustrating what may be called the social aspects of the Resurrection, so far as it contains a revelation of our relation to the world around us, and of the character of that Church which is the divine witness and embodiment of its truth.

CHAPTER III

THE RESURRECTION AND THE CHURCH

Willst du ins Unendliche schreiten,
Geh nur im Endlichen nach allen Seiten.

GOETHE.

1. IN the preceding chapters the Resurrection has been viewed in two main aspects. At first it was contemplated as a fact, standing in the centre of the development of human life, and adding a new element to the sum of the records of human experience. It was then contemplated as an idea, harmonising conflicting instincts of man's nature and lifting him into a real communion with a nobler order of beings by an abiding fellowship with the unseen. So far the Gospel of the Resurrection vindicates its claim to a true historic basis and a moral fitness for meeting the essential needs of men. But it has a yet wider application. It offers a new foundation for social union. It is not only a message of salvation to the individual: it is also the pledge of a divine life to the Church. The promise of Redemption, symbolised by the deliverance from Egypt, prefigured by the types of the law, illustrated by the teaching of the Prophets, was the vital bond of

the people of Israel; and no less the accomplishment of Redemption, shown in the Resurrection, the Ascension, and the consequent Mission of the Comforter, is the spring of life in the Christian Body. In the Church the fact of the Resurrection, so to speak, is perpetuated; and the idea of the Resurrection is realised. On the one hand, the development of the Church witnesses to the consecration of every power of man to a divine use, and marks the potential transfiguration of every variety of individual or national character as parts of a sublimer whole; and on the other hand it claims the possession of this transforming energy in virtue of the working of a Risen Saviour through its outward institutions. Briefly it is inherently historical and sacramental; and the clue to the apprehension of its history and its sacraments lies in the Resurrection.

2. The detailed examination of the institutions of the Church in the light of the Resurrection is at present impossible (compare i. § 61). It will be sufficient to consider how the fact and the idea of the Resurrection affect the general conception and working of the Christian Society. Nor can the consideration be regarded as superfluous at the present time. Some strange forgetfulness of truth must prevail when it can be possible for philosophical writers to stigmatise Christianity as "selfish." The very same Gospel which sets before the single believer the glorious issue of life, at the same time and by the same message binds up his hope with that of every other believer, and more than that, with

the destiny of the whole world. It is only by neglecting the Resurrection that the Christian can be isolated (compare i. § 1).

3. "The first announcement of the Gospel connects it with the establishment of a society. It is emphatically "the Gospel of the Kingdom." "The Kingdom of heaven is at hand" was equally the message of the Baptist and of Christ Himself at the beginning of His teaching. At one time this Kingdom is contemplated as still future, at another as already present. We are taught to pray for its "coming," and encouraged to press as it were by force and claim by violent effort a share in its immediate blessings. Its origin, its growth, the manner of its reception, the perils to which it would be exposed, the variety of elements which it would include, are portrayed under a rich variety of parables. "I appoint unto you that ye may eat and drink at My table in My Kingdom" were among the last words which the Lord addressed to His disciples; and after His Resurrection, during the forty days, He spoke "of the things pertaining to the Kingdom of God." The idea which was thus prominent during the ministry of Christ was included in the groundwork of the Apostolic preaching. The first address of St. Peter on the day of Pentecost declared "Jesus to be the Lord and Christ" Whom God had promised "to raise up to sit on the throne of David." The first record of a mission beyond the limits of Judæa describes Philip

Matt. iv. 23.
Matt. xi. 12; Luke xvii. 21.
Matt. xiii.
Luke xxii. 29.

"preaching the things concerning the Kingdom of God." The definite charge which was brought against St. Paul when he first preached in Europe was that he did "contrary to the decrees of Cæsar, saying that there is another King, one Jesus."

Acts xvii. 7. Compare xvi. 21.

4. It is unnecessary to consider the various misconceptions to which this proclamation of Christ's "Kingdom" was exposed. Even to the time of the last manifestation of the Lord on earth before the Ascension, the Apostles seem to have confounded "the Kingdom of God" with that which was its figure, "the Kingdom of Israel." But there is not the least trace that the Christian idea of a heavenly kingdom was ever mixed up with direct political aims. The very bitterness with which the Jewish zealots at the time of their rising persecuted the Christians, is a sufficient proof that these "children of the Kingdom" were as far as possible removed from schemes of temporal ambition. The Christian belief did away with the bitterness of civil bondage, and substituted a higher hope for the dreams of national enthusiasm. But none the less the Kingdom whose coming believers were charged to hasten, was regarded as a society truly answering to the name, though its establishment was referred to the action of Divine Providence, and not to human design. The kingdoms of the earth were types of this kingdom which should be on earth though not of the earth. In other words, the glorious society in which the Gospel was to find its outward embodiment would have a

Acts i. 3, 6.

Sovereign, of whose Personal Rule His subjects would be conscious and by Whose Will they would be guided, an organisation, by which the relative functions and duties and stations of those included within it would be defined and sustained, a common principle of action, and common rights of citizenship. This was the earliest form under which the establishment of a Christendom, at first militant and then triumphant (though this distinction was but faintly perceived), was realised. The old Kingdom of GOD whose history could be traced in the Old Testament furnished the language in which it was described, and the wide-felt presence of the Roman Empire gave distinctness to the broader traits of universal dominion and unity.

5. But the idea of a Kingdom was not the only one under which the Church—the whole society of Christians—was regarded. "Thou art Peter (*Petros*)," our Lord said, in answer to the confession which the great Apostle had made, "and on this Rock (*Petra*, the living rock, from which the *Petros* is hewn or taken) I will build My Church." This then is a second figure: the Church is a building, or more specially a house or temple. And it is worthy of notice that St. Peter, in his first Epistle, brings out this conception into the clearest light. "Ye," he writes, "coming to the Lord, a living stone, . . . as living stones are built up a spiritual house," of which "the stone which the builders disallowed is made the head of the corner." And St. Paul yet more in detail

Matt. xvi. 18.

1 Pet. ii. 4, 5, 8.

follows out the structure of this Christian sanctuary. Reckoning up the blessings of the Gentile converts, he tells them that they are now "fellow-citizens of the saints . . . since they have been built upon the foundation of the Apostles and prophets, Jesus Christ Himself being the chief corner-stone, in whom every part of the building, fitly framed together, groweth unto an holy temple in the Lord; in which ye also are builded together for an habitation of God in the Spirit." It is, however, to be observed that the same image which is used of the society is used also of the individuals. We are "Christ's house," "God's building," "the temple of the living God," where the words are used of the many to whom or in whose person the Apostle is speaking; and on the other hand he asks, "Know ye not that your body is" (in each separate case; or better perhaps, according to another reading, "your bodies are") "a temple of the Holy Spirit which is in you?"

Eph. ii. 19-22.

Heb. iii. 6; 1 Cor. iii. 9; 2 Cor. vi. 16.

6. This figure of a Temple has several points in common with that of a Kingdom, from which it is distinguished in its essential scope. In both there is the design of the whole to which the parts are subordinated, a variety of office and position in the constituent elements, a central power on which the stability of all depends. But there is no necessary connection between the Temple and Him Who dwells within it, such as is implied in the reciprocal duties of governor and governed. The house may be defiled or desolated, while the occupant

seeks some other abode; but the King is such in virtue of his special sovereignty. Briefly, the Temple prefigures the Church in its outward fabric, in its splendour, in the vastness of its plan, in the variety of materials of which it is constructed, in the consecration of all which men have to GOD by men and so through GOD by His Presence. It is the material as contrasted with the moral type of the Christian society.

1 Cor. iii. 10 ff.

7. But there is yet another image under which St. Paul presents the relation of the Church to GOD. It is not only His Kingdom, and the Temple of the Holy Spirit: it is also the Body of Christ. Our Lord indicated this vital connection between Himself and His disciples in the parable of the Vine and the branches; and after His Death and Resurrection the truth thus signified grew plainer and more prominent. It was seen that Christians had not only severally works to do, but different works: they were felt to be not branches merely, but members of Him from whom they drew their life. So it is that this idea of the Church as the body of Christ includes in itself both the idea of the Kingdom and that of the Temple. Sovereignty and organisation are implied in the Headship of Christ, and in the mutual action and dependence of the members: external structure and multiformity and consecration, in the framework of the body, and in the variety of its parts, and in the relation of the whole to the vital Spirit by which it is informed. But it also adds much to the ideas which it thus harmonises. The connection

of life is substituted for that of government or occupancy. We live in Christ, and He in us. We grow in Him; and He is seen more and more perfectly in the society of Christians. The government of a society shows something of the character of the ruler: the fabric of a building something of our conception of him for whom we rear it; but the body reveals in part the very person of him whose it is, and is the organism by which alone his acts can be manifested or fulfilled.

8. We are not perhaps justified in pressing the details of these three images in an examination of the general characteristics of the Christian Church. The images indeed are by no means always kept distinct. Language borrowed from one is used in the development of another. "Ye . . . are built up a spiritual house . . . ye are a chosen generation, a royal priesthood, an holy nation, a peculiar people." The gifts which Christ has variously distributed among men are "for the building up of His body." "Know ye not that your bodies are members of Christ? . . . Know ye not that your body is (*or* bodies are) a temple of the Holy Spirit which is in you?" One relation runs into the other, just as in all other cases we stand in threefold connection with Him who created, redeemed, and sanctified us. But without insisting on the minute interpretation of the figures, so much at least is evident, that they mark the Church as ruled by a personal Governor, possessed of an outward organisation, inspired by an immediate divine life. What light then,

1 Pet. ii. 5, 9.

Eph. iv. 12.
1 Cor. vi. 15, 19.

it may be asked, does the Resurrection throw upon the nature of this Kingdom of GOD, this Temple of the Holy Spirit, this Body of Christ? for it is with this subject only that we are immediately concerned.

9. "My Kingdom," our Lord said, in answer to Pilate, "is not of this world." And yet He added presently, "Thou sayest [rightly] that I am King. For this purpose have I been born, and for this cause have I come into the world, that I may bear witness to the Truth. Every one who is of the Truth heareth My voice." The Resurrection was the passage to the proper realm of truth—of that which really *is*; and in the contemplation of the Resurrection the Christian learns something of things as they are in the sight of GOD. The Resurrection is a new birth: to realise it as an actual fact with the consequences which it involves, is to share in it; and thus we gain the full meaning of Christ's words to the Teacher who seemed to boast of the insight into spiritual things which his training had given him: "Verily, verily, I say unto thee, Except a man be born again, he cannot *see* the kingdom of GOD"—he will have no faculties to apprehend that which it contains. Plato, in one of his grandest myths, has represented the progress of unembodied spirits in the train of the gods in the face of all that *is*. When they fall to earth, as their powers fail them in their course, their destiny is determined by the clearness and extent of the impressions which they retain. These recollections form the

John xviii. 36, 37.

John iii. 3.

Plat. *Phaedr.* p. 247.

basis of all that men know of truth. The Christian reverses the idea. He is going to a kingdom of absolute Truth, and is not fallen from one. The Resurrection is the bridge by which the passage to the unseen is effected. Resting on that he looks out to the heavenly state of which he is a citizen: he feels the constraining force of his allegiance to a spiritual King: he apprehends something of the divine hierarchy, to a fellowship with which he is admitted, and according to whose laws he works: he sees the enemies against whom he has to contend, "principalities, and powers, and rulers of the darkness of the world, and spiritual wickedness in the heavenly realm." The order, the scene, the persons, the objects of this spiritual kingdom, answer to what we see now on earth, but no more. A new heaven and a new earth await the manifestation of Christ, even as men themselves will be transfigured by His presence (ii. §§ 47, 48).

Eph. vi. 12.

10. It is obvious that there is great danger in dwelling exclusively on this royal aspect of the Church. It is likely that in such a case either the relations and duties of men on earth will be neglected and disparaged, or conflicts and differences here will be absolutely confounded with those which are essentially spiritual. History furnishes many examples of both errors. "The Kingdom of God" has been the watchword equally of those who have cast aside the restraints and claims of life, and of those who have sought to mould its form by the most merciless fanaticism. And it was perhaps in

part due to their vivid anticipation of Christ's Return with kingly majesty that the early Christians took so little interest in civil affairs. Yet this cannot justly be turned to their reproach; for it must be remembered that in the Roman Empire politics, as we understand the word, had no place; and Christianity, as such, has no special relation to any one form of government. In the long run it tends to certain social results, but in virtue of its universality it is capable of the highest personal development under any outward circumstances.

11. But the Church is not a Kingdom only. It is a structure complex and multiform. The society as a whole is a dwelling-place of the Holy Spirit. It is reared from age to age by the accumulated efforts of all who serve GOD. Each brings that which he has of special worth, and it is built into the fabric. All work is not the same work, yet all which can bear the presence of GOD is equally employed in some part or other of the spiritual "building." If the notion of a Kingdom suggests the essential majesty of the Church, this of a Temple brings out the human interest of its progress. So it was with the structure which suggested the image of St. Paul. "Forty and six years was this Temple in building," and it carried with its foundations the memories of ten centuries. So it is with our Christian Temples which combine and hallow the thoughts and gifts of successive ages. And the spiritual reality answers to the material figure. The Church is itself the record of its history:

1 Cor. iii. 12.

John ii. 20.

it is a monument and a shrine. Each race, each nation, each century, nay, each faithful workman, has left some mark upon it. Time gradually harmonises parts which once seemed incongruous. Additions which were at first thought to mar the symmetry of the plan are felt at a later period to increase its richness. One Spirit hallows all, and that Spirit is a gift consequent on the Resurrection. The local withdrawal of Christ from among men in the one limited form in which they had known Him, and the transfiguration of that form "by the glory of the Father," were the conditions through which they could realise His unseen presence through the Spirit. "It is expedient for you that I go away," the Lord said to His disciples on the eve of His departure; "for if I go not away, the Comforter will not come unto you; but if I depart, I will send Him unto you." He first wakened their souls to the perception of His new Life, and then removed all which might still seem to confine its manifestation. "Cling not to Me," was the loving reproof to her whose eyes he had opened by a familiar word, "for I am not yet ascended to My Father." No love, however true, which sought to keep Him as He was seen on earth, could know the fulness of Christ's majesty. The Ascension was the necessary completion of His work. So only could men trust in His abiding power ever testing, and receiving and consecrating the many offerings of every generation, and using all in due measure for the service of that society in which He was pleased to dwell.

John xvi. 7.

John xx. 17.
Rom. vi. 4.

12. So far we have touched upon those aspects of the Church which represent its eternal constitution and its temporal growth. The Resurrection gives force and distinctness to both. But it is more especially in the last figure of the Church, as the Body of Christ, that it finds its peculiar application. The idea which this figure expresses springs indeed properly out of the belief in a Risen Saviour. Anticipations of the idea are found in the later discourses of Christ which have been already noticed; and elsewhere He spoke of His continual presence among men in the persons of the poor and of His ministers. But these and other intimations of like kind fall far short of the full grandeur of the conception which St. Paul lays open. Nor can it be without significance that the revelation is made to us through him who was resolved not to know "a Christ according to the flesh," and to whom the Lord was first manifested in the majesty of His divine glory. The Church is (if we may so speak) the visible Body of the Risen Christ: it is through this that He still works, in this that He still lives.

2 Cor. v. 16.

13. Three principal relations are included in this conception of the Church as the Body of Christ. Christians as such are essentially united together in virtue of their relation to Christ, and that irrespective of any feeling or will of their own. Next they are bound to one another by the obligation of mutual offices, the fulfilment of which is necessary for the well-being of the whole. And lastly, all alike derive

their life from their Head Who is in heaven. The Body is one: it is multiform; and it is quickened by a power which is not of itself but from above. Now this element in its constitution, now that, is brought into prominence, but none can be neglected if we wish to form an adequate notion of its power and functions. For the present it will be enough to consider a little more exactly the principle of unity, and that in which the unity consists, the principle of life. The multiformity of Christendom will be noticed sufficiently while we endeavour to establish its unity.

14. Before doing this, however, it may be well to notice how the fundamental idea of Christianity as the basis of a society is related to the corresponding ideas of Judaism and Paganism. It has been frequently argued that modern civilisation has lost some essential element of good which ancient civilisation possessed. It has been said that we are less self-reliant than the nations of classical antiquity: less conscious of a Divine Presence than the Jews. Without pausing to inquire whether this is so in fact or not, we may be contented to ask whether there is anything in Christianity itself which tends to produce such a result: whether the evil or loss, if it be actual, is also necessary.

15. The noblest lesson of Paganism is without doubt the revelation which it makes to us of the inherent dignity of human nature: of the powers of endurance

and self-denial and faith: of the perceptions of beauty and truth: by which the soul is at all times capable of asserting its divine relationship. The work of Paganism was, we are led to believe, the complete exhibition of these natural faculties, in their strength and in their weakness. The nobility of man as man and as standing apart from God is that portion of its teaching by which it still appeals most forcibly to the sympathies of our own time. There is a dark side to the picture which we are apt to forget, but still there is an abiding grace and manliness in classical life as it is seen in history and literature and art. Unaffected interest in every human feeling, many-sided culture, stern and indomitable will, claim our respect and awaken in us responsive efforts. But so far as we admire Paganism there is nothing in Christianity antagonistic to it. Paganism closed its eyes to suffering and death. Christianity takes account of the whole nature of man, of its good and its evil, and justifies in the face of the contradictions of life the instinct which affirms its dignity. It looks death face to face not as an inevitable necessity but as a final consequence of sin, and yet realises even now more than a victory. It lays bare, what each one must feel for himself, our natural infirmity, and yet ratifies the bold words of the heathen poet that "men are God's offspring," and sets before believers as the aim of their faith a more complete "fellowship in the divine nature." It represents life as a struggle, and yet as a struggle only to realise the blessings which are already won for man and within

Acts xvii. 28.
2 Pet. i. 4.

his reach. It claims his entire homage, but at the same time it consecrates to its own service the natural exercise of every power which he possesses, and the fulfilment of every situation in which he is placed. It looks upon the world as suffering with him, but it regards it no less as destined to share his glorious future. It differs from Paganism as a whole differs from a part. It takes up into itself and harmonises with the rest of our experience the isolated truths to which Paganism bears witness.

16. This is equally true of the relation in which Christianity stands to Judaism. If Paganism is a testimony to the self-assertion and independence of man, Judaism is the confession of his dependence. In the first we contemplate man in himself: in the other man as the creature of God. In Paganism, at least when it reached its full development, an appeal is made to a common conscience, or to necessary laws of thought, or to history: in Judaism the binding message is "the Word of the Lord." In the one men obey, because they recognise the essential justice of the command or submit to a stronger force: in the other the statutes of right are not primarily based on intuitions or suggested by experience, but embodied in a Law which is absolute, not in virtue of its inherent character, but as coming from Jehovah. The one, if we look to the principle by which it lived, is a witness to human freedom: the other to Divine sovereignty. And as the principles which they respectively embody are eternal, so are the

spirit of Paganism and the spirit of Judaism. The history of Christianity is little more than the history of the approximate harmonisation of the two. Now the solution turns in this direction and now in that, according as the spirit of Greece or of Rome prevails—the theology of Athanasius or of Augustine—but Apostolic Christianity recognises and hallows both elements. The coming of the Lord invests humanity, even as it is, with a more awful majesty than man could have claimed for himself; and at the same time connects the realisation of that majesty with the direct revelation of the Divine Will. Paganism proclaims the grandeur of man: Judaism the supremacy of God. Christianity accepts the antithesis, and vindicates by the message of the Resurrection the grandeur of man in and through God.

17. This then is the work of Christianity, first to establish the common dignity of men as men, and to place on a sure basis all purely human virtues; and next to connect the life of men with its source and consummation and bring it into fellowship with God. Both these results are grounded on the historic facts of the Gospel. The unity of the Christian Society, to which potentially all men belong, depends not on any personal feeling, but on a common relation in which men as belonging to the society stand to God. And the reality of this divine fellowship is at once the seal of the nobility of man and the pledge of the possibility of its final perfection.

18. "As the body is one," St. Paul writes, "and hath many members, and all the members of the[1] body being many are one body: so also is Christ. For in one Spirit we all were baptized into (*i.e.* by baptism incorporated in) one body, whether we be Jews or Greeks, whether we be bond or free; and were all made to drink[2] one Spirit." Here the unity is seen to spring out of a definite outward act, and the participation in a spiritual blessing consequent upon it. No other conditions are added. Yet it must be observed that according to the formula which Christ Himself enjoined, Baptism includes a profession of faith, such as has been connected with it in all ages, in which the historic facts of the Lord's Life are plainly set forth. Hence in another place St. Paul says more fully: "There is one body, and one Spirit, even as ye were called in one hope of your calling: one Lord, one faith, one baptism." The act once done brings with it, in virtue of Christ's work, fellowship with Him, in which lies unity. "Know ye not that so many of us as were baptized into Jesus Christ, were baptized into His death? Therefore we were buried with Him by baptism into death; that like as Christ was raised up from the dead by the glory of the Father, even so we also should walk in newness of life." Here the issue is viewed from the human side. It is ours to realise in action the fulness of the heavenly life of which we are made partakers. Elsewhere it is viewed in relation to God, and in this aspect all is

1 Cor. xii. 12, 13.

Eph. iv. 4.

Rom. vi. 3. 4.

[1] Omit *one*. [2] Omit *into*.

accomplished once for all. "When we were dead in sins [GOD] quickened us together with Christ, and raised us up together [with Him], and made us sit together in the heavenly realm in Christ Jesus."

Eph. ii. 5, 6.

19. The participation in Christ's Death and Resurrection through Baptism is then the final condition of unity: to work out the Resurrection in life the means and measure of its preservation. For unity is not uniformity. Differences of race, class, social order, obviously have no influence upon it. They are of earth only. But more than this, it is consistent with serious differences in the apprehension of the common faith on which it reposes. St. Paul naturally insists on the removal of the partition between Jew and Gentile by the Death of Christ, whereby He "made of twain one new man." Primarily without doubt he regarded the contrast as it was before the Gospel; but it seems equally certain that he included within the scope of Christ's reconciliation those diversities of opinion by which the Jewish and Gentile Churches were separated. The Apostles of the circumcision recognised in him the apostolate of the uncircumcision; and he gladly received from them "the right hand of fellowship." The divergences of practice between the teachers, and of belief to a certain extent between the disciples of the two schools, were not sufficient to destroy their true unity. Love still found its expression among them in acts of charity. It was only when the attempt was

Eph. ii. 15.

Gal. ii. 7 ff.

Gal. ii. 10.

made to enforce one partial system as universal that the unity of the whole was endangered. The first serious effort to establish uniformity threatened to end (as it did after the time of the Apostles) in a schism.

20. It may not indeed be a mere fancy to regard the manifold appearances of the Lord after His Resurrection as prefiguring in some way the varieties which should exist in after time in His Church. The unity of His Person was not in any way impaired, and yet He showed Himself to His disciples in different "forms." And it may be still that the faithful eye can see a Body of Christ where His Presence is hidden from others. For even in the one body, there are many bodies; and as the whole Church is sometimes contemplated in its completeness as distinct from Christ, though most closely bound to Him, as His bride; so also is the same true of separate Churches. "Ye are a body (*not* the body) of Christ, and members in particular," St. Paul says to the Church of Corinth. The definite article destroys the force of his argument. And so again in his second Epistle: "I espoused you"—the congregation to which he is writing—"to one husband, that I may present you as a chaste virgin to Christ." Thus the whole is not only relatively complete, but it is made up of parts (so to speak) similar to itself. And this is true if we regard even the ultimate members of which it is composed. The individual Christian—a temple of the Holy Spirit as well as a

Mark xvi. 12.

Eph. v. 27.
Apoc. xxi. 2, 9.

1 Cor. xii. 27.

2 Cor. xi. 2.

living stone of a more glorious Temple—is like the special Church of which he is a member, even as this is like that Universal Church in which it discharges some special function.

21. But while the Christian, the separate Churches, and the Universal Church have severally, in some sense, a completeness in themselves, yet their real life is solely in their connection with Christ "the Head of the man," and "the Head of the Church." From Him flows that energy by which every member is enabled to discharge its function effectually and in due proportion to the harmonious working of the whole: from Him, that power of love by which the several parts are fitted and knit together: from Him, that vital force by which the multiform body "increaseth with the increase of GOD." Each phase of this divine Life is distinctly marked. "The bread"—the heavenly manna—"which I will give," the Lord said, "is My flesh, for the life of the world."—"Because I live, ye [My disciples] shall live also"—"I am the Resurrection and the Life." "Ye died," St. Paul writes to the Colossians, "and your life hath been hidden with Christ in God; but when Christ is manifested, our Life, then shall ye also be manifested with Him in glory." "It is no longer I who live," he says in another place, "but Christ liveth in me." "He that hath the Son hath life; but he that hath not the Son of GOD hath not life."

1 Cor. xi. 3. Eph. v. 23. Eph. iv. 16. Col. ii. 19. John vi. 51. John xiv. 19. John xi. 25. Col. iii. 3, 4. Gal. ii. 20. 1 John v. 12.

22. It is then necessary to bear two things in mind in treating of the Unity of the Church. The Unity of the whole is consistent with a wide variety of parts, each having to a certain degree a corresponding unity in itself. And next, the essential bond of union is not external but spiritual: it consists not in one organisation but in a common principle of life. Its expression lies in a personal relation to Christ, and not in any outward system. Of the life of the Church part is open, part is hidden. We can see divisions, differences, limitations; but all that is eternal and infinite in it, all that controls actions which perplex us and harmonises discords which are unresolved to our senses, is not to be perceived on earth, but is with Christ in heaven.

23. It follows necessarily from what has been said that external, visible unity is not required for the essential unity of the Church. To recur to the example which has been already used, the congregations of Jewish and Gentile Christians were no less One in Christ, though the outward fellowship between them was imperfect or wanting: their common life lay deeper than the controversies which tended to keep them apart. Their isolation was a proof of imperfection, but not of death. What errors are deadly, it does not fall to our part to attempt to determine. It is enough to observe that differences of opinion which were once thought by many to be fatal to unity were really consistent with it. The promise of Christ does not reach to the unity

of the outward fold at any time. "Other sheep," He said, "I have, which are not of this fold: them also I must lead, and they shall hear My voice; and there shall become one flock, one shepherd"—one flock in however many folds it be gathered, because it listens to the voice of the One Shepherd.

John x. 16.

24. If the true unity of the whole Church, which is derived from the participation in the Spirit of Christ, is compatible with the existence of outward divisions on earth, it is no less compatible also with the existence of independent centres of local and partial authority in its manifold organisation. Christ Himself is the One Head; and He left no single successor to represent in outward form the relation in which He stands to the Body. For a time indeed an idea seems to have prevailed in one province of Christendom that the office of Christ (if we may so speak) and not of the Apostles only was to be perpetuated. The Jewish Bishops of Jerusalem, who were taken as long as might be from the family of the Lord, were held by many to be (even though they did not claim the title themselves) His successors. They were, according to the title claimed for them, "bishops of bishops." Their authority, as far as can be learnt now, was supposed to extend over the whole world, and not to be confined to a single diocese or district. They symbolised the idea of an earthly kingdom, which was characteristic of the party who professed to maintain their opinions.

It would be idle to speculate on the form which this belief might have taken if Jerusalem had not been destroyed. As it is, it is impossible not to feel that the effect of the desolation of "the Holy City" must have been to chasten and purify (as soon as they could bear the discipline) those who had hoped to mould the Christian Church after the pattern of Judaism. The conception of unity based on a historic and divine succession in the religious centre of the world was proved to be no part of the true idea of the Church. The thoughts of men were turned with a deeper faith to that "Jerusalem which is above," to which from the first St. Paul had directed them.

25. These considerations tend to remove a difficulty which has been often felt in dealing with the interpretation of the New Testament. The Apostles, it is urged, looked for an immediate "end of the world," and the event shows that they were in error. Yet to any one who really penetrates below the surface of the first age it will be equally evident that "the end of the world" was expected, and that it really came. It is possible that the Apostles themselves, like the prophets in earlier times, did not realise the mode in which their expectations would be fulfilled: it is certain that many who heard them affixed false and chimerical interpretations to their teaching; but in the light of Christian history their written words were fully accomplished. The destruction of Jerusalem is "the meeting of the ages," the death of the "old world," and the birth

of the "new world." The Lord "came" when the acknowledged centre of "the people of GOD" was desolated. A spiritual and universal Presence was substituted for a material and local Presence. The lesson of the Resurrection replaced the lesson of the Law. A fresh "age" (*æon*) began its course destined itself to culminate in another "coming" of which the first was a living figure. In a religious aspect all things were essentially become new. Christianity had first vindicated its inheritance in the past, and then in due time it asserted its independence.

26. The outward unity which was aimed at in the early Jewish Church was based upon a religious idea. The outward unity which afterwards grew up round the Roman Church sprang from political influences. The two systems are essentially distinct in their origin, though finally they can be traced in theory to the same principles. The Roman system became in the end what the Jewish system was from the first, but with one remarkable difference. The priesthood, which was in both cases the visible representative and instrument of the theocracy, was limited in Judaism to a distinct family succession: in Romanism the succession was spiritual and effectually disconnected from hereditary ties. In the Christian Church of Jerusalem the fleshly descent from a sacred stock was observed for several generations, but there is no trace of a similar custom at Rome. The idea of spiritual supremacy seems indeed absolutely to exclude it. But it must be enough to

have indicated the external contrast between systems essentially similar. This is not the place to follow out the steps of their parallel but converse development. Nor can we dwell on the marvellous process by which the Roman Church was prepared for the preservation of Christianity on the dissolution of the Empire. It would be foreign to our purpose to trace the steps by which the bishop of the imperial city received one by one the prerogatives of sovereignty, and in due time seated himself on the vacant throne of the Cæsars. It would be equally out of place to attempt any estimate of the strength which the mediæval Church thus received for the execution of the work with which it was charged. The facts are of vast significance, and occupy so large a space in the history of Christendom that they may not lightly be passed over. They formed, as we may well believe, part of the providential scheme of the historical growth of the Church. But the unity to which they led was no necessary part of the constitution of the Church. It answered to the one Empire of the first age, and not to the many kingdoms of the maturer life of Europe. It supplied a bond between the disorganised nations till the states-system into which they were formed was firmly consolidated. Under its protection the Romanic and German elements were allowed to gather strength till they were ready to fulfil their independent office. But without dwelling upon this temporal function of the external unity of the Christian society, we can at least see from the fall of its prototype after the Jewish

Return (i. §§ 27 f.) that the spiritual unity of the Church is independent of it. The outward unity arose from historic causes: it was broken by historic causes. No external organisation can supersede the original relation in which the Society stands to its Founder. The gift of the Holy Spirit was the outward sign of the elevation of humanity to glory at the right hand of God: the sharing in that gift is the life of the Church: the absolute oneness of the source from which the gift flows is the ground of essential unity in the congregations of which the Church is composed.

27. But though the principle of the unity of the Christian Church is spiritual, and not necessarily connected with uniformity of constitution, or even with intercommunion, it by no means follows that the outward organisation of the whole of the constituent Churches is a matter of indifference. On the contrary, the direct teaching of the Resurrection points to the inherent connection between the outward and the spiritual, the organisation and the life. The range of variation in the constitution of the Christian societies must be limited by their fitness to embody the fundamental ideas of Christianity. Of this fitness history on a large scale gives the final judgment. Whatever may be the immediate result of controversy, however false may be the issues on which it is decided, however blinding the influences by which its progress has been modified, in the end it is seen in its true light, and the final judgment which is ratified by general practice or

belief is commonly the true one. In this sense history is the arbiter not of truth but of the right embodiment of truth. The early records of the Church are little more than the records of conflicts which once seemed doubtful; but in each case that which had in it the element of permanence lived on, and Catholicity stood in full strength against the broken forms of partial and erroneous teachings.

28. It is possible, perhaps, to extend this view of a historic development of Christianity to later ages. It seems difficult to believe that the Greek and Latin Churches include the only two great aspects of Christian truth, so that it remains for us at present only to recur to the principles on which they were built, and to strive vainly to reproduce in another period a transcript of the past. The vast advances of civilisation, the further growth of national life, the wider range of knowledge, which brings with it the recognition of the importance of special views, seem to force upon us the conviction that the various Churches of modern times fulfil under the changed conditions of society the same functions as could be discharged in earlier times by a single Church. Even in the history of Judaism something of the same kind may be noticed. In no way, as we should judge, could the possibility of variation, and still more of division, be excluded with greater certainty than by the institutions of the Jewish Church, and yet in that Church outward union was soon broken, and the rupture, if not expressly sanctioned, was in the end implicitly

accepted by the divine prophets of Israel. Israel was "made to sin," and yet even so while their primal sin remained they were not abandoned by GOD. The Temple—the permanent (i. § 25) symbol of unity—was hardly completed before a large part of the nation was shut out from the use of it. The political and religious schism of which Israel was a monument was not passed over without rebuke, but in spite of that a distinct spiritual work was carried on in Israel, not less blessed by outward signs than that which was simultaneously accomplished in Judah. At a later time the office which was discharged by the Jews of the Dispersion, and specially by the Alexandrine Jews, in modifying and extending their traditional faith, was still more manifestly recognised by GOD in the providential office which He allowed it to fulfil for the spread of Christianity. Here as elsewhere it appears as if the sins and wilfulness of men gave occasion to the accomplishment of the Divine plans. These indeed were not dependent on such evils for their fulfilment; but yet it seems as if GOD were pleased to use our imperfections for the complete exhibition of His will. The rebellion of Israel, the schism of Alexandria, the permanent settlement of Jews throughout the East and West, which involved a violation of large parts of the Mosaic law, were in themselves evils, and had their spring in selfishness and disobedience, but none the less they served to work out a vast counsel, which, as far as we can see, could not otherwise have been perfected. Thus in the history of that earlier kingdom of GOD, which was essentially outward, we are taught by special examples not to judge everything by our own standard of unity. And at least no argument can be drawn from the circumstances which attend the rise of any great movement against the importance of the part which it may have to discharge in the furtherance of the purposes of GOD.

29. But it may be said that such a view sanctions sectarianism. If we are to suppose that the form of the Christian Church in each nation will (within certain limits) embody the common peculiarities of national character, just as on a larger scale the Greek Church is Orthodox and the Latin Church Catholic, differences will still exist in the body thus formed. Each nation will include men most widely at variance in their religious tendencies. Are they then to be held blameless if they seek to attach themselves to a communion which expresses most clearly their own views? The national character is not reflected in them; and the same general principle which justifies the formation of a separate national Church may be appealed to in support of an indefinite number of subordinate associations.

30. Disregarding for the present all considerations of ecclesiastical organisation, it may be sufficient for us to answer to such a line of reasoning that it applies equally well to all social combinations. No one will deny that there is a tendency in every nation towards the establishment of the government best suited to it. This tendency, which may be latent in the mass, though really

there, will be developed most strongly in those who are the true leaders of popular thought. And though various obstacles may hinder or modify the embodiment of the idea which they represent, in the end it finds an adequate expression. But even then individuals in the state will find themselves at variance with the constitution. This divergence, however, will not release them from the duties of loyal obedience, nor yet deprive the government of its right to be regarded as the representative of the national feelings. The state, though made up of individuals, has an existence of its own. The individual will exercise his full influence in preparing for further changes, but meanwhile the whole claims a sacrifice of the part. It is so also in the case of a national Church. No general principles can be laid down to justify a schism or a revolution. The future alone can decide on the sufficiency of the alleged causes from which they arose. And in many cases the issue which is sanctioned by experience may have been occasioned though not caused by selfish motives.

31. In the history of the Church no less than in the history of nations we have to deal with humanity in which sin is active already. It would be easy to show that among perfect men every blessing would arise naturally and completely without conflict or division, which in our present state is realised through these exceptional means in pain and at best partially. But as it is, conflict and sorrow are the means by which

the powers of men, material and moral, are braced and purified. The existence of distinct nations with rival interests is practically necessary for the full development of those special powers in each which holds out the surest promise of a final union of men. And so the antagonism of separate societies of Christians serves not as the best, but as the most appropriate discipline for bringing out the manifold applications and capacities of the one Gospel.

32. History has in fact sanctioned divisions in the Christian Church whatever we may think of the events which first led to them, or of the actors by whom they were made. However deeply we may deplore the loss of that outward fellowship which would, if it could have been preserved, have increased a thousandfold the power of the Church upon the world; yet it is impossible not to feel that God has revealed His purposes and furthered His work not only in spite of, but even through the separate societies which have severally appropriated this or that part of the whole truth as the characteristic object of their devout study. And even without regarding the lessons of the past, it is hard to see how the fulness of Christianity could have been manifested among men otherwise than by antagonism and conflict. Antagonism is in our present imperfect condition the preliminary to our apprehension of anything which is not itself absolutely bounded by our finite powers. Every spiritual truth can be followed out to a final antithesis; and this antithesis finds its

most complete expression in societies rather than in individuals.

33. The same law which holds in all other fields of human activity, holds also in the noblest. The condition of advance in the comprehension of the whole Gospel is the special mastery through the circumstances of life of its constituent parts. Progress implies a separate development of powers. The tendency to division grows as knowledge widens. There was a time when all nature seemed to lie within the range of one mind. Deeper inquiry has shown that each fragment includes phenomena which may occupy a lifetime. And so it is in religion. The complexity of modern society, which is in part a creation of Christianity, lays before us endless problems of right and duty, and opens countless avenues for the entrance of truth into the manifold life of men which could not have been presented if all the conditions of existence had been similar. As a necessary consequence of this, each nation, each association, each man, has, in proportion to the distinctness of character, a tendency to do one thing; and the tendency to do it springs (as a general rule and upon a large scale) from the fitness for doing it. There is thus, in virtue of the universality of Christianity, a constant approximation towards the complete manifestation of its power. And when each age and race and individual has fulfilled its proper function—and so far as it fulfils it—a glorious harmony must result, which is true Catholicity.

34. The recognition of some such historic development of Christianity, varying according to the wants of particular ages or races, as belonging to its present form, restores to the divided Churches a true unity. One of the earliest images under which the unity of Christendom was described was that of many streams flowing from one source. The longer the streams flow, the greater will be their divergence ; but the divergence is due to progress, and does not in any way destroy the original unity of the waters which pass along the various courses. But the streams will not always be divided. They start from one source and they end in one ocean. They have been united outwardly, and they will again be united. Meanwhile the fashion of their currents is moulded by the country through which they pass, and this in turn furnishes the peculiar elements which they bear down to their common resting-place to form the foundations of a world to come.

35. There is indeed much of human selfishness in the present administration and conduct of Christian societies, even as there was in their establishment and organisation. It is not argued that the divisions as we see them are not deformed by much that is unchristian. They are a witness to human imperfection ; but at the same time they show how the failings of man are overruled to the furtherance of his highest destinies. They belong to an order of things in which sin is realised and not only possible (ii. §§ 23 ff.); but they are made an occasion during this brief time of trial for the salutary

discipline and fruitful development of powers which cannot yet be harmoniously concentrated on one end. On the whole a fictitious unity is more destructive of vital energy than partial dismemberment, for it tends to weaken the striving after essential unity. The disruption of the visible Church was a calamity which still impedes its action, though even thus, as by the fate of Jerusalem, we are taught to look above for the source of the one life by which its parts are seen to be inspired. The petty rivalries of the day are an evil, though they are an evil which may be borne. But the line of thought which has been opened leads to a trustful and reasonable view of Christendom. It enables us to regard the progress of the Church as we regard the progress of civil society (§ 38). It encourages us to extend our sympathies beyond the limits of our own communion: to look forth without despair upon a world, in part hardly reached by the very sound of Christ's message, in part divided as to the exact meaning of it. It teaches us to watch with patience the slow and painful and wavering advance of truth through long ages, as falling in with what we observe in nature of the enormous scale and gradual progress of the accomplishment of the operations of GOD (i. §§ 2, 3). The example of the Jewish Church, the legible chronicle of past centuries, shows that under circumstances similar to those which exist now, though simpler and narrower, He wrought out His work, and used the fruits of man's wilfulness and one-sidedness for the accomplishment of His designs. So we trust it will be now, and in confidence we can fulfil the task which we find ready to our hands, without distrusting the means placed within our reach for furthering the coming of the Kingdom of Christ.

36. Some law of development Christianity must have. The Christianity of the first age, regarded as a whole, is not the Christianity of any later age; and no view of the Church can be complete or satisfactory which does not include and explain the principle of the change. It is impossible for a Christian of to-day to date the descent of his faith from any critical epoch in modern times, and neglect ten or fifteen centuries as a mere parenthesis in the history of the Catholic Church. All the past is included in the present. The Reformation was the fruit of ages gone by no less than the germ which should spring to maturity in ages to come. There can be no suspension in the fulfilment of the divine promise, however varied may be the forms under which it is accomplished. The leaven still works in the manifold mass: the seed advances stage by stage towards its ripe perfection: the tree grows under every change of season and climate, and offers shelter to all who repose beneath its branches. Each image under which we are taught to contemplate the function of the Church presents at once an element of permanence and an element of change. There is the essential life by which the whole body is quickened, absolutely one and immutable, and the organisation which the vital force moulds and by which it reveals itself, which is mutable

and fashioned out of elements earthly and transitory. But even so the continuity of the organisation is necessary for the preservation of the complex life.

37. The principle of life is one and immutable. In this there is no development. The faith which is written in the facts of the Gospel, and the immediate Apostolic interpretation of them, admit of no necessary and authoritative additions. A dogmatic development of Christianity, in the sense of an increase of the fundamental doctrines of the faith, is foreign to the whole spirit of the Apostolic writings, and is itself inconceivable without a new revelation. Such a development would only take place by the addition of new dogmas in virtue of the direct action of an adequate power, or by deductions from existing dogmas. But both methods are excluded by the nature of the case. Christianity rests essentially on facts. Its elementary doctrines are presented to us in the shape of facts; and thus, even if any central power existed with absolute dogmatic power, new facts would be required for the basis of new doctrines, for the Apostles declare with unmistakable distinctness the full significance of the Incarnation and the Mission of the Holy Spirit. And again, the truths which answer to the facts of the Gospel belong in themselves to a higher form of existence, and cannot be brought within the domain of our powers of reasoning. Every process which we pursue involves necessarily at each step limitations (as, for example, of time and space) to which the Divine Being is not subject. Every

conclusion, therefore, which we form, so far as it is presented as an absolute truth, must have in it an element of error. Indeed, on reflection, it cannot but seem infinitely presumptuous that we should venture to speculate on that of which, even in its simplest form, we can give no positive conception. Nor is there any characteristic by which the Apostolic writings are more clearly distinguished from the greatest writings of masters of theology than the absence in them of secondary deductions from the principles which they enforce. In this respect they differ equally from the metaphysical and speculative theology of the East, and from the moral and legal theology of the West. They contain a record of facts and an immediate application of the facts, but no more: life and not thought is the object to which they primarily minister, and so they minister (as no other writings ever could do) to thought through life. They set forth with simple distinctness *that* a fact or truth is, but not *how* it is or *why* it is. What there is more than this in later speculations, however beautiful and however precious it may be, is wholly different in kind. From the first the difference has been instinctively felt. The records of the most critical struggle for the truth in the history of the Church show how widespread was the unwillingness to introduce into the historic creed of Catholic Christendom a single word which was not found in the Scriptures, though it was the necessary exponent of their teaching in opposition to error: the language of the noblest champion of orthodoxy shows how far he was willing to dispense with the acceptance of a word when the fact which it imperfectly expressed was admitted.

38. But while the principle of life, the record of the facts of the Gospel, remains the same, the form in which it is embodied may change. Thus we naturally turn to history as showing the conditions and ruling the mode of the development of Christianity. Here we can see on a large scale how the same truths are apprehended by different races, how they are embodied under different circumstances and according to different modes of thought, how they conquer, and array themselves in the spoils of the conquered. No one would deny that in successive ages special aspects or parts of Truth are brought out. The general outline of the history, including both the history of dogma and the history of practice, has a necessary connection with that of civil and intellectual history. The one is, so to speak, a function of the other. And it follows that as we can trace in the general condition of man a constant advance towards a true fulfilment of the capabilities of his nature, so we may hope for a corresponding progress in the Church, towards that ideal which is held before us in Scripture as its proper consummation. Advance in the first case is not only consistent with wars, revolutions, isolated action, but (as far as we can judge) is even dependent on these which we are tempted to call hindrances in its way. And it may be so with Christianity. The divisions and rivalries and heresies and schisms by which the Church is torn may be means towards the fulfilment

of its office. As we look back we can scarcely doubt that it is so. The storm no less than the sunshine is needed that the rainbow, the visible token of God's covenant with man, may be seen upon the cloud.

39. It is indeed impossible to regard the Church as a body without recognising the necessity of a constant change in its organisation. Growth itself is change; and in proportion as the life of the body is complex we may expect the forms in which it is clothed to be varied. There are times when the individual is forgotten in the society, and conversely when the society is forgotten in the individual. In the Apostolic view of the future of Christianity there is a distinct recognition of a progressive work in both. The life of the Church is continuous even as the life of the man; but with this difference (as we have seen, § 20), that this life is manifested not in one outward embodiment, but in many, which are severally similar to the whole which they combine to form.

40. It is no part of our task to attempt to follow out in detail the various phases of the life of the Christian Churches. But it would not be difficult to show that institutions or dogmas have wrought a most important work for the cause of Christ in one age, which in another have been converted into obstacles to the full apprehension of the Truth. There is always a great danger that

that which has been found of critical use at one time will be pronounced necessary for all time. Mistaken gratitude changes the outward means of deliverance into an idol. The organisation through which the spirit once worked is reckoned holy, even when the spirit has left it. And thus that which once was a development of life becomes a corruption, not because it has (in every case) changed in itself, but because it stands in a different relation to the whole. The work of the mediæval Church (for example) required modes of operation which could not be retained now without a faithless neglect of the lesson which God has taught us in the last four centuries. The same phenomenon meets us at every step in the economy of individual life. The seed from which rises the fruit-bearing tree, to which the visible society of Christendom is likened, gives birth to a thousand successive organisations, from the seed-leaf to the flower, which fall away when their peculiar office is fulfilled. They perish, but their work remains, and remains because they perish.

41. This consideration brings with it the answer to a general objection which may be urged against the belief in a divine historical development of Christianity. It may be said that the development is due to the imperfection of man: that so far from carrying forward the perception of the Truth, he lowers the truth to his own level, and confines it in a form borrowed from his own weakness. The objection is true if it be directed to any particular point of the development. The Truth itself

is infinite, and it is simply because the powers of man are imperfect and finite that any development is necessary. He can only realise step by step, and by successive efforts, what *is* indeed from the beginning.[1] According to the position in which he finds himself, he takes now this, now that fragment of the whole, because it meets his wants. Every embodiment of the Truth must be wrought out in this way. And the nearest approximation which we can form to the complete truth is by the combination of the partial realisations of it which history records. The imperfection of each stage of the development is then only perilous when an attempt is made to transfer the forms of thought or practice of a particular period to another, without any regard to their bearing upon the whole life of the time. The interpretation of Ecclesiastical history, like the interpretation of Scripture, is based upon a proportion. Neither admits a rigid literalism. The training of the child and of the man will be different, if both are according to the same law; but the man may learn still (if he reads them rightly) from the lessons of the child.

42. It is not denied that there will be a tendency in man not only to seize that element in the Truth which he himself needs, but also to exaggerate its importance, to array it in fancies of his own, to transmit his embodiment of it as an inviolable heritage to all who shall

[1] Augustine's enforcement of this truth in one of his most pregnant passages is full of interest: *Enarr. in Psalm.* xliv. 5.

come after. If it were not so, superstition would have no vitality. But while we look to history for the record of the continuous growth of the Church, we carry the Holy Scriptures with us, as the test whereby to try the essential value of each development. The history of the Old Covenant is enacted afresh in the history of the New. The fulness of the Apostolic writings has not yet been exhausted in the life of eighteen centuries. The providence of GOD is at every stage interpreted by His Word. The spirit of the Resurrection tries and transfigures each transitory embodiment of Truth.

43. The same test which is applied to the past history of the Church can be applied to the present. The vast complexity of modern life, the various degrees of national culture, the broad differences between class and class in the same nation, set before us simultaneously, so to speak, distinct periods of the simpler life of the ancient world. We live (and the statement is not a mere figure) in the presence of many ages. We cannot be surprised then if we see around us many Christian societies distinct, and subserving in virtue of their distinctness to distinct types of thought and feeling. Differences which once were found in the same external body are now seen embodied in separate societies. We lose something by the change, but the gain must not be neglected. We are led to look for the spiritual basis of unity instead of reposing in the fact of formal unity. And more than this. The full development of each part is best secured by independent action. Division (if we regard the im-

perfection of our nature) appears to be the preliminary of that noblest catholicity, which will issue from the separate fulfilment by each part in due measure of its proper function towards the whole. Thus the material unity of Judaism is transformed into the moral unity of the Apocalypse. The unity which was at first spontaneous becomes at last conscious, tested in all its elements and made perfect by conflict.

Eph. iv. 16.

44. It has been urged against this view which leads directly to the recognition of national Churches as a providential mean towards the complete exhibition of Christianity, that national Churches are "contradictory to the nature of a religious body" and "opposed to the genius of Christianity." If Christianity were of this world only, a simple organisation for social and political discipline, the objections would be true. But they fail because the Church *is* a religious body, partially manifested on earth but drawing its life from an unseen source, and one because that source of its life is One. In this respect the idea of the Church may be compared with the idea of humanity with which it is potentially commensurate. The existence of separate and conflicting nations is not destructive of the moral unity of the whole body of mankind, but rather on a large view is seen to minister to its external realisation in the long succession of ages. And so with the Church, though in this case the unseen principle of unity is far more easily apprehended, the distinct embodiments of partial sections of it tend to bring about in the end that complete

development which will answer to the fulness of its divine life. The separate Churches thus become as individual members in the larger body, and, like single men themselves, contribute, by the most distinct preservation of their individuality, to the perfection of the whole. In the light of the Resurrection all the powers of man in their most free combinations are capable of transfiguration.

45. But it will be obvious that this division of Churches, like the division of nations, is only a transitional phase in the whole history of humanity (compare § 26). It belongs not to the early but to the later stage of its development. Nay, rather, if the history of the ancient people of God may be taken as a type of the progress of the new "world," it appears to be the latest stage in the evolution of "the present age," and to precede a more immediate revelation of the Divine Presence. However this may be, the faint recognition of national Churches is not a mere "resource in the face of overwhelming difficulties," but a testimony to the power of Christianity to find for itself new organisations to meet new phases of society. Meanwhile we can be content to find in this diversity of operations scope for the most devoted energy and the firmest faith. It has been nobly said that "nations redeem each other." One supplies that which another lacks in moral character and purpose; and the existence of a deficiency in one place is not unfrequently the stimulus and the occasion for the display of the

corresponding virtue in another. At least it is evident that we cannot understand how, with our present powers, the full grandeur of humanity could be exhibited or developed except by the coexistence of many peoples distinct, and even antagonistic. And that which is true of humanity in a political or social aspect is true of it also in a religious aspect. Separate organisations appear to be as necessary for the complete manifestation of the many sides of Christian truth in relation to man, as they are confessedly for the manifestation of national life. But we do not rest in the contemplation of a divided humanity or of a divided Church. Under the varieties of race and character there exist tokens of an essential union which may yet be realised and towards which the current of events is ever turned. There are indications, faint it may be and often baffling, of a common life grander than the life of men and the life of nations, which is struggling to assert its sovereignty. And in the Church there is yet more than this, the certainty of the presence of a Holy Spirit who "is able to subdue all things unto Himself." But whether we look to nations or Churches, it is needful that we should pause before we claim to exercise the prerogatives of a knowledge which belongs to a higher sphere. As citizens and Christians we stand in varied relations to a universe of which we can see but the least part. This world is not all; and if we look confidently for a unity of the whole, we dare not attempt to construct it in imagination upon the little field which is open to us.

46. The forms which present divisions assume are, it is admitted, and must remain, causes for the deepest sorrow. Nothing can be more grievous than the partial wilfulness with which Christian men and Christian societies exalt from time to time with an idolatrous devotion special fragments of truth, which tend to lose their essential character by being isolated. But such reflections as have been suggested, while they leave the special evils of a divided Christendom just as they are, yet enable the devout mind to regard them without despair : nay, more, to regard them, as it would regard the disorders of the physical world, with quiet confidence and faith. We cannot yet see how the whirlwind or the earthquake falls in with an infinitely benevolent system of nature; but we do not doubt that it does do so. In looking on human life we have even better grounds for faith. There we can see faint beginnings of a final harmony, converging tendencies towards a divine order, which will embrace all the varieties of thought and life in their richest fulness. When we see what the belief in Christ and the power of His Resurrection has done, how it has interpreted and made its own this and that instinctive feeling, how it has found an embodiment, natural if not complete, under every variety of external circumstances, how it includes in itself a principle of unity capable of combining whatever there is in these of permanent value, we can look out upon the conflict of sects without distrust, and look forward to that golden age *to* which and not *from* which the history of the Church advances.

47. Nothing is more paralysing than a sense of isolation: nothing is more cheering than a consciousness of fellowship in the combined action of a great nation or of a great society. Christendom is weak not only because it is divided, but chiefly because each section is enfeebled by a sense of the littleness of its power as it measures the triumphs of Christianity by its own peculiar standard. Our strength will be indefinitely increased if we believe that God works not only through us or in our way and according to our notions, but uses us according to the measure of our capacities, and others with us in the accomplishment of the design of His Love. Every energy will be turned to its proper work as our thoughts rest on the glory of the Risen Saviour.

48. Wherever we look the first question which arises is ever: To what purpose is this waste? On all sides we see a prodigal wealth of powers which to us appear to pass away without effect, of germs of life which never fulfil what we think to be their proper destiny, of beauty which gladdens no human eye. In the moral world the same mystery recurs. One man out of many, one family of many, one nation of many, one world of many (if our thoughts dare wander so far), are centres of blessings of which all are equally capable of sharing, and we cannot trace the law by which their influence gradually reaches to the farthest limits of being, while we see multitudes perish unconscious of

their common heritage. All nature teaches the same lesson. "We know in part." It is enough. If Christ be risen, in that fact lies the pledge of "the restitution of all things" towards which men are encouraged to work.

Acts iii. 21.

APPENDIX I

ASPECTS OF POSITIVISM IN RELATION TO CHRISTIANITY[1]

ὃ οὖν ἀγνοοῦντες εὐσεβεῖτε τοῦτο ἐγὼ καταγγέλλω ὑμῖν.
Acts xvii. 23.

Catéchisme Positiviste, ou Sommaire Exposition de la Religion Universelle. Par AUGUSTE COMTE. Paris. 1852.

Système de Politique Positive, ou Traité de Sociologie Instituant la Religion de l'Humanité. Par AUGUSTE COMTE. Paris. 1851-1854.

I

No religion can fail to be a fruitful subject of study: even the rudest reveals something of the natural feelings and wants of man which are awakened by the experience of life. And exactly as we believe Christianity to be *the* Truth, we shall confidently expect to find in it all that is true in the manifold expressions of human thought. Thus it has happened not unfrequently that independent speculations or instinctive aspirations have brought out elements in the Gospel which had been before overlooked or set aside. They were there, and even actively at work, but they were not consciously apprehended. And so it seems to be now. The religion of Positivism is offered as the final result of a profound analysis of society and man, and its unquestion-

[1] This essay originally appeared in the *Contemporary Review*.

able attractiveness to pure and vigorous minds indicates that it does meet with some peculiar force present phases of thought. Are there not then lessons which we may learn from it?

While I endeavour to answer this question, I shall be content to take Comte's own conclusions, without discussing the processes by which he obtains them. The strength of the Positivist philosophy lies in its method; the strength of the Positivist religion lies in its conception: and the Positivist alone is concerned with reconciling the two. That which is at best only a hypothesis for the Positivist may prove to be a reality for the Christian; and while I set aside the physiological basis of the Positive religion, it need scarcely be said that I do not propose to deal with the principles of Positivism as furnishing a method of philosophy. I desire simply to explain what Comte lays down as the essential bases of religion, from an exclusively human point of view, and to consider whether his exposition throws any light upon neglected aspects of Christianity.

But though this is not the place to discuss the philosophic aspect of Positivism, one remark is unavoidable. It seems to be generally assumed that there is some fundamental antagonism between the Positive method and Christianity. Nothing, I believe, can be more false. I should even venture to maintain that the spirit of Positivism is more in harmony with a *historic* religion than that of any other system of philosophy. It knows nothing of causes, and consequently decides nothing prior to observation. It refuses to recognise absolute laws, and consequently is always ready to take account of new facts. As against a metaphysical theism the arguments of Positivists may perhaps avail; but they are inherently powerless against a faith which is based, not on subjective theories, but on outward events, of which all personal experience and all social development furnish the adequate and only conceivable verification.

This being so, it is evident that a Positivist in philosophy may be a Christian in religion; and the religion constructed on Positivism may, as far as it goes, illustrate or confirm the doctrine and constitution in which the Church has embodied the facts of the Gospel. How far this is so is the subject with which we have now to deal. And with this problem before us, it would be superfluous to criticise the errors and misrepresentations—to use no harsher terms—with which Comte's religious writings are disfigured. He puts them forward so boldly and so frequently, that no one moderately conversant with Christianity can be misled by them.[1] It is equally unnecessary to exhibit his weaknesses. Others, who have dwelt on these with more than necessary detail, have paid the penalty of becoming blind to what there is really noble and just in his teaching. And it is with this that we are concerned. A system is formidable, not by what there is false in it, but by what there is true in it. If then it can be shown that Christianity assures what Positivism promises—if it can be shown that it includes in a fact what Positivism symbolises in a conception—if it can be shown that it carries on to the unseen and eternal the ideas which Positivism limits to the seen and temporal—we may be sure that Positivism will have no lasting religious power, except as a transitional preparation for a fuller faith. Comte will be one more in the long line of witnesses who show that the soul is naturally Christian.[2]

[1] Something has been said in a former paper on Comte's fundamental misconception of the idea of Christianity, *Contemporary Review*, vi. 417 ff.

[2] In this unconscious prophecy of faith, Comte offers a singular parallel to the great poet of the Roman Republic. Both were bitterly hostile to the established faith of their countries. Both sought to lay in the study of nature the firm basis of human life and hope. Both were profoundly impressed with the sense of the unity of the world,

II

To some, however, it must seem strange to speak of any system as a religion which does not recognise the action of a Personal God. For us indeed the idea of religion is so naturally connected with that of theology, that it requires a serious effort to separate the two. A perfect religion must indeed take account of three elements—the individual, the world, and God; but an imperfect religion can exist, if the individual recognises without him an infinite power, contemplated as personal, and such as to claim the complete devotion of the worshipper. The Great Being of Comte—the sum of all humanity, past, present, and future—practically satisfies the condition of infinity; and it satisfies the condition of personality by the concession which is made to each worshipper to represent it to himself under some definite historical or imaginary type. In fact, we may be driven to ask ourselves whether the Being which some Christians worship is less truly an abstraction than the idealised humanity of the Positivists.

But while we must never leave out of sight, in dealing with the Religion of Positivism, the fundamental defect which mars its completeness, it is necessary to remember that this is not the only form in which a religion can be founded upon a dualism, though it is that most repugnant to our instincts. Dr. Newman, in a striking passage of

But, in spite of the similarity of the moral position of the two teachers, we feel that they are separated by more than eighteen Christian centuries. Lucretius sought in the explanation of the origin of things that confidence which Comte looks for in the observation of their being. The one feels his way towards the intellectual conception of a harmony of nature; the other, towards the moral law of the discipline of life. Both, as it seems, were heralds of a crisis of thought. To both the Resurrection is the complete fulfilment of aspiration and teaching.

his *Apologia*[1] has sketched the permanent influence of evangelical teaching upon him, which consisted in "confirming me," he says, "in my mistrust of the reality of material phenomena and making me rest in the thought of two, and two only, supreme and luminously self-evident beings—myself and my Creator." Thus, as Comte leaves out the Deity from his elementary conceptions, another school leaves out the world. A little reflection will show that a system based upon either dualism is irreparably though not equally imperfect. The one passes into Secularism, the other into Mysticism; while the fulness of Truth springs from the co-ordination of both.

There can be no doubt that the quotation from Dr. Newman expresses the popular view of the constituent elements of religion, though this personal antithesis is more truly characteristic of Protestantism than of Roman Catholicism. It is therefore easy to see in which direction the study of the Positive religion is likely to be fruitful to us. By dwelling on the relations of man to humanity and to the world, Comte has again vindicated for religion its social destination. Since the Reformation, the general tendency of religious influences has been to individualism; and thus a bold and exclusive enunciation of the complementary aspect cannot but contribute to the restoration of the true harmony between personal and social religion which Christianity, as we believe, alone contains.

III

Having thus indicated the one vast lacuna in Comte's theory of religion, and the manner in which his system is

[1] P. 59. It is, however, difficult to judge whether Dr. Newman himself holds this to be the final analysis of the elements of religion.

likely to supplement other popular theories, we may proceed to trace the outlines of it as he has drawn them. "Religion is," he says, "the complete harmony proper to human existence, individual and collective, when all its parts are brought into due relation to one another."[1] It is for the soul, in other words, what health is for the body;[2] and as health is essentially one, though in all cases variously and imperfectly realised, so too religion is essentially one, though it is attained in various forms and in different degrees. Even to the last, it is an ideal to which each specific type is an approximation.[3]

The object of religion, corresponding to this definition, is set forth as twofold. It is destined at once to discipline (*régler*) the individual, and to unite (*rallier*) the separate individuals in a harmonious whole. It aims at personal unity and social unity.[4] And the same influences which tend to correct the selfish instincts of each man, tend at the same time to bring all men into a true and lasting concord.[5]

And as the aim of religion is twofold, so also is its base. It reposes on an objective and on a subjective foundation.[6] Without, there is the external order, in itself independent of us, which necessarily limits our thoughts and actions and feelings. Within, there is a principle of benevolent sympathy, which prompts us to look beyond our own wants

[1] *Politique Positive*, ii. 8. Compare *Catéchisme*, p. 2. "[Religion] indique l'état de complète *unité* qui distingue notre existence, à la fois personnelle et sociale, quand toutes ses parties, tant morales que physiques, convergent habituellement vers une destination commune."

Thus Comte adopts the derivation from *religare*, and not from *relegere*, which Augustine also defends: *De Vera Religione*, 55; *Retract.* 13 (the whole of this revision is full of interest).

[2] *Pol. Pos.* l. c.

[3] *Pol. Pos.* l. c. *Cat.* 3.

[4] *Pol. Pos.* ii. 66. *Cat.* l. c.

[5] *Pol. Pos.* ii. 10.

[6] *Pol. Pos.* ii. 12, 17, 25. *Cat.* 28.

and wishes, and to seek in a wider harmony the satisfaction of the deepest instincts of our nature.

The same dualism is extended also to the composition of religion. It has an intellectual part and a moral part. The former includes the adequate conception of the general laws of physics, of life, of society, to which our feelings and our actions are subordinated. The latter, under the shape of discipline, regulates our conduct at once public and private, and, under the shape of worship, guides and intensifies our feelings. Briefly, the sphere of doctrine is thought, and its end is the True; the sphere of discipline is action, and its end is the Good; the sphere of worship is feeling, and its end is the Beautiful. And, as a whole, religion teaches us to know, to serve, and to love the great Being, in whom all that falls within the range of our power is summed up.[1]

IV

In this view of the character and scope of religion, which no one can deny to be grand and comprehensive, even while it lacks the Christian elements of infinity and personality which we necessarily crave, one point is of commanding importance. Religion, Comte tells us, is the bringing into harmony the order without us and the spirit within us; the last and perfect combination of faith and love.[2] This conception is the true key to his whole system. Our chief work, therefore, is to learn the character of the bases on which these final principles respectively repose.

On the one side then we have a vast external order, of which a fuller knowledge is gradually unfolded in the long course of ages, whereby we apprehend it as within certain

[1] *Pol. Pos.* ii. 19 ff. [2] *Pol. Pos.* ii. 16.

limits at once fixed and variable. Step by step we are forced to contemplate the phenomena which it presents as falling into groups, and connected with one another by certain relations of sequence. The laws of observation which we thus form are extended gradually from physics to life, and from life to history, till we feel that not only are the ages permeated by "an increasing purpose," but that all being also is united by one principle. The efforts of Reason—and the juxtaposition is important—naturally culminate in the nobler efforts of Faith.[1]

This order is apprehended, as has been said, as being both fixed and variable; and in both respects it affects us beneficently. The fixity furnishes a solid basis for our thoughts and actions, and, by making foresight generally possible, saves us from idle speculation and from misdirected energy. At the same time it sets an impassable limit to personal caprice, and, by basing all life upon submission, prepares men for sympathetic effort as united in obedience to a common supremacy.[2] Its variability, on the other hand, is the pledge of progress. It stimulates speculation by suggesting a series of problems of surpassing interest. It guides activity by opening fields for labour, and substituting fruitful obedience for passive resignation. It represses at once asceticism and mysticism by offering its greatest blessings not to personal, but to social labour.[3]

Such, according to Comte, is the objective base of religion. On the other side, it is observed that there is an internal tendency in man, springing from benevolent affections, which carries him beyond himself in the search after his

[1] *Pol. Pos.* ii. 25 ff. p. 17. "L'état religieux repose donc sur la combinaison permanente de deux conditions également fondamentales, aimer et croire, qui, quoique profondément distinctes, doivent naturellement concourir. Chacune d'elles, outre sa nécessité propre, ajoute à l'autre un complément indispensable à sa pleine efficacité."

[2] *Pol. Pos.* ii. 28 ff.

[3] *Pol. Pos.* ii. 37 ff. *Cat.* 16, 41.

proper happiness and dignity.[1] Just as the laws of the external world are only slowly and partially made known, so this inner life is brought out by the gradual evolution of society. The love of the Family passes into the love of the State; and the love of the State rises into the all-embracing love of Humanity.

This tendency also, like the external order, is at once fixed and variable. In some shape or other, it will make itself felt in every man. It may be dwarfed and neutralised by atrophy, or strengthened and ennobled by exercise. But in its normal development Love spontaneously apprehends by moral intuition what Faith systematically constructs by intellectual processes; and at the last both coincide in their complete fulfilment. Faith sees the harmony of all things, which Love feels.

Nor may we forget that while the ultimate objective and subjective bases of religion are thus broadly distinguished, there is yet always a human element in our conception of the Cosmos, and a cosmical element in our feelings as men. The unity of the world is subjective.[2] The laws of phenomena are gained by the abstraction of the constant part from the variable. And conversely, the development of love is objective. It gains strength only as it is manifested according to the conditions of our existence. Man indeed is himself, according to the wise instinct of old philosophers, a microcosm, including in his own person the action of all the laws which we observe without us, and supplementing them by that higher law of love whereby he alone is capable of religion.[3]

According to this exposition, it is evident that religion is built upon knowledge, and the Positivist system of doctrine is simply the outline of the hierarchy of the

[1] *Pol. Pos.* ii. 14.
[2] *Pol. Pos.* ii. 32 f. *Cat.* 36, 77.
[3] *Cat.* 95, 122.

sciences, which are severally subordinated one to another, and each regulated by its peculiar laws. In due succession the believer or the student—for the words become synonymous—learns to appreciate the universal laws of number, time, and space, by which all our definite conceptions are ruled; next he passes to those of physics, which are more complicated and less general; then to those of chemistry, which brings him to the verge of life. The investigation of the laws of life leads to that of the laws of society; and the last and crowning science in this scheme is that of morals.[1]

Such an encyclopædic review of the great departments of knowledge reveals two important principles. Each science is based upon those which precede it in the scale, so that in every case the nobler phenomena are subordinated to the lower. And, secondly, each science, as it increases in complexity, admits also of greater variations.[2] To these principles two corollaries may be added. First, that each series of laws produces its full effect in every instance, though the result may be modified by the action of new forces acting according to new laws. And, again, that the power of foresight, which measures the definiteness of the law, varies from absolute certainty in the case of combinations of number, and the like, to indefinite doubt when we speculate on the isolated action of individuals.

V

One important conclusion follows from this mode of

[1] The connection of the sciences is clearly given, *Pol. Pos.* ii. 58 ff. The most complete examination of their distribution and relations is in *Pol. Pos.* iv. 187 ff.

[2] *Cat.* 50, 70, 73. Thus many phenomena will never be brought under definite laws.—*Cat.* 52.

viewing the relations of religion and science, which has been commonly lost sight of by physicists no less than by theologians. If it be true, and it seems to be incontestable as far as it goes, a conflict between religion and science is impossible. Not only are the two subjects heterogeneous, but the results of science—whether physical or human—are part of the data which it is the function of religion to co-ordinate.

Moreover, if we complete the great hierarchy of the sciences by the addition of theology above morals, it is obvious that the same principles will hold good. The new science, so far as it deals with facts, will never be independent of the action of the forces revealed by the lower sciences; but it is not itself shaped by them. In dealing with it, we shall have to take account of new forces manifested under new laws, which may modify in a manner wholly inconceivable before experience the laws and forces of the lower sciences; but theology is no more, therefore, inconsistent with them than the science of chemistry, for instance, is with the science of life. It is impossible to anticipate from the observation of an inferior science what will be the phenomena of another above it; and, conversely, the phenomena of every superior science will be subject to the laws of those below it, though they are not explicable by those alone. A problem in biology cannot be solved by the application of chemical laws, though these must be considered in dealing with it; and so also a question in morals cannot be dealt with solely by laws of life, or a question of theology by laws of ethics; though, in both cases, the subordinate laws underlie the final result.

Thus the Positive view of the dependence of religion on science errs by defect, and not in principle. It requires to be supplemented, and not overthrown. And when the whole cycle of human thought and experience, of consciousness as well as of observation, is brought within the range of scientific study, we are first capable of perceiving the full grandeur of the idea of religion. Its destiny is not only to discipline (*régler*) and to unite (*rallier*), but still more to reunite (*rélier*). It is the final harmony of man, the microcosm, not with the world alone, but with God.

It is of no moment in this respect what view we may take of nature (*natura, werden*). Every fact in science furnishes new material for religion, and at once enlarges its scope and tends to define its character. But, that it may do so, no fact must be looked at by itself. At present science suffers at least as much as religion from partial and contracted views. The student of physics perpetrates as many solecisms as the student of theology. Every one would feel the absurdity of a geometrician denying a fact in morals because it is not deducible from his premisses; and yet it is not a rare thing to hear some explorer of inorganic nature gravely argue that nothing can be known of God, because his inquiries give no direct results as to His being or His attributes. Thus each partial observer of ethics, or history, or nature, is tempted to forget that there are other phenomena than those with which he deals, and so to use his fragmentary laws as measures of the universe. The degradation of science is the inevitable consequence. But when all observed facts are placed in their proper categories, whether they be facts in physics, or biology, or social science, or ethics, or theology, they will, as we believe, teach us something more of the will of God, which is made manifest to us, according to the nature of the subject-matter, in the several orders of being with which each of these departments of knowledge is respectively conversant.

We claim then, by our Christian faith, that the sphere of religion be recognised as coextensive with the utmost bounds of human thought and knowledge, while at the same time it is dominated by a moral purpose which springs from sympathy or love. The personal object of religion—the reconciliation of man to God—is not likely ever to be absent from our minds; but there is at all times a tendency to omit, at least in popular exposition, this complementary view of the harmonisation of man with humanity and nature. Scepticism at once occupies the ground which is abandoned. And in this lies one of the great lessons of Positivism, that by asserting religion to be the complete harmony of man and the Cosmos, it has forced again upon our notice aspects of Christian truth which have been more or less hidden since the teaching of the greatest Greek fathers was superseded in the West by the necessarily narrower system of Latin theology. Some conception of the great order at present we must have;[1] and if our religion is, as we believe, the highest expression which can be given to faith and love, it will embrace this also. We shall rise beyond the individual standing-point to some one higher and more commanding; and while we retain firmly our original sense of the inestimable worth of the individual soul, we shall feel also that each is part of a sublimer whole, extending through all time and space, and bound by sensible and indissoluble links to the sum of all being.

VI

It is not difficult to characterise the ideas which are brought into prominence by this extension of the religious field of life. The Positivist suggests the ideas of continuity, solidarity, and totality; the Christian, going yet further, adds the idea of infinity; and without the distinct recogni-

[1] *Cat.* 26.

tion of these four ideas, it seems to be impossible to represent adequately the message of Christianity, as a historical and sacramental religion, to our own age.

A very little reflection will show the profound influence which continuity exercises upon life. When it is once apprehended, no religion which claims to be universal can neglect it. Materially, intellectually, and morally, we are the children of the past, destined in turn to give birth to a new race which will inherit all that we possess. Whatever view we may take of the originative power of the individual, and we claim necessarily that the personal will shall be admitted to be an independent force, it is evident that the accumulations of wealth of every form which furnish the instruments of our action, the treasures of language which control the general tenor of our thoughts, the forms and habits of social and national intercourse which stimulate and guide our feelings, are incomparably stronger than any individual power which can be brought to bear upon them. If it were not so, in place of society we should have chaos. And all these are in their source and growth independent of us. We can watch how, in old times, the various results of labour and reflection and conflict were gathered up and perpetuated in abiding shapes; but we have no choice but to receive them. It is our privilege to modify, but not to begin. More and more as the ages go on, in Comte's striking phrase, we who live are ruled by the dead, though it is our prerogative to serve them with a free and willing service, and in our turn, when our work is done, to be joined with them in the sovereignty of the future.[1]

Two important conclusions flow from this law of our earthly existence. The first is, to borrow again Comte's

[1] *Pol. Pos.* ii. 61. *Cat.* 32. The question of hereditary character deserves more attention from moralists than it has received. Cf. *Cat.* 102.

own phrase, that progress is the development of order;[1] and the second, that the thoughts or institutions of the past can be applied to the present only by a method of proportion.

As to the first, it is of no moment whether, like the Positivist, we regard the phenomena of society simply in themselves, without referring them to any higher cause, or whether we see in them (as we do) the manifestation of the will of God. No one looking back over the past can fail to detect a general advance of humanity, as a whole, in certain definite directions corresponding to what we observe in the fuller development of the man. The progress, on a large scale, exhibits the harmonious elevation of our whole complex being, even though periods of devastation and fiery trial are needed for the preparation of the future growth.

The second consequence, though it is really more obvious, is more commonly overlooked. Any expression of popular judgment, whether it be made by word or by act, is necessarily relative to the time and circumstances under which it is made. As circumstances change, it does not by any means follow that the changes in the acceptation of words or in the significance of acts will be made in the same direction, so that the relation between them will remain fixed. And therefore, if we would gain for ourselves the blessings which we can refer in past ages to certain institutions or formulas, it can only be by realising the relation in which they stood to the whole constitution of society then, and finding their proportional representatives now. To transfer a form of one age unaltered into another is in most cases to be faithless to that very principle of continuity by which we claim to be children of the first century, or the fourth, or the ninth, or the thirteenth. We

[1] *Cat.* 108.

are the children of the men who lived then; we cannot be the men themselves.

The doctrine of solidarity is not less fruitful of thought than that of continuity. It presents to us (if such an illustration is allowable), in a horizontal section a similar succession of varieties of society to that which we have considered before in a vertical section. Or, to take another mode of expression, it presents in the extension of space what continuity regards in the extension of time. In a family, or a city, or a nation, we can readily apprehend how the coexisting members are bound together so as to form a whole, of which each part is really, though remotely, united to the others by material and moral actions and reactions. Our observation of the subtle influences by which continuity is preserved helps us to extend this idea yet further. Nation is thus seen to be moved by nation, stock by stock, till the whole race, which is connected spiritually by a community of nature, is felt also to be connected actually by mutual, though often indirect, operations of each fragment upon the rest.

Whenever we seize, however tremblingly, as at best it must be, this vast conception of the Great Being in which all mankind is for the time united, it is evident that our views of the destiny, of the relations, and of the action of men will be greatly influenced. The thought which inspires hope and assures patience at the same time ennobles labour and stimulates action. Hope and patience spring necessarily out of the application of the lessons of the past to the present. We can see how rivalries and conflicts, the rise and fall of principles and states, the very exhaustion of powers once beneficent and life-giving, have contributed to the whole progress of human life. We can believe then that phenomena of the same kind, when coexistent, are no less instrumental of good. And it is no objection to this faith that it is not in our experience converted into sight. Life would be indefinitely impoverished if the fruits of effort or suffering were not reserved in the richest measure for the future.

The present effect of the idea of solidarity upon labour and action is perhaps less frequently realised than the remoter effect which has been just noticed, but it is at least capable of being far more energetic. Briefly, it may be summed up in two principles. It consecrates the permanent variety of functions in life,[1] and substitutes duties for rights.[2]

As long as we regard individuals as so many separate units, it is clear that we must regard complete equality as the ultimate ideal of their state. The object of reform must be to assimilate man to man. But this chimerical fancy loses all rational basis when the individual is seen to be the member of a body which itself is part of a greater whole, of which the final dimensions surpass all human imagination. Then it follows at once that complexity of office is the condition of health. The completeness of health depends on the completeness of the organism. Society, in every true sense, would cease to exist without an abiding distinction of classes. Humanity would be poorer if it were deprived of any national or specific types. There is no confusion in the multiplicity of service. There is no levelling, no disparagement, in the just subordination of distinct works. The essential variety, the actual combination, both belong to the characteristics of life.

[1] *Cat.* 109, 113.

[2] *Cat.* 289. The conception of salary as simply designed "à remplacer chez chaque organe social les matériaux qu'il consomme toujours, comme provisions pour sa subsistance ou instruments pour sa function" (*Cat.* 116), is worthy of attention, as well as the principle on which it is based, that "chaque service personnel ne comporte jamais d'autre récompense que la satisfaction de l'accomplir et la reconnaissance qu'il procure" (*Cat.* 117).

And if we apply the principle to the separate work of each, it becomes, as it were, a revelation of the moral dignity of labour. No one in any society works for himself. Each worker is a servant of the body. He does really co-operate with all for the good of all. It is only required that he should feel the destination and the source of what he does and of what he receives. Then at last he would, as Comte admirably expresses the truth, know that "to live *for* others" is but another aspect of "living *by* others."[1]

At the same time the transference of our point of sight from the individual to the body brings out into clear light the second principle. If the individual be the centre, then he may have rights; but if the body be the centre, he can have only duties. It is possible that these complementary aspects may be reconciled, but there can be no doubt which we most frequently forget. And if we once add the Christian idea of what the body potentially is, all notion of personal claims vanishes in comparison with the infinite debt whereby we are bound, each in our measure, to fill up that which is lacking to the completeness of the whole.

The doctrine of what I have ventured to call the totality of life carries yet one step further the doctrines of its continuity and solidarity. It is not only that the successive generations of men are linked together by laws which they can only modify, and not abrogate, nor yet that each generation is interpenetrated and united by a common life; but the life of humanity is itself ruled, in a great measure, by the medium in which it is passed. The influence of physical powers upon man may have been exaggerated, but we cannot deny that it is real. Comte himself does not overstate it. "The world," he writes, "furnishes the materials, and man

[1] "Vivre pour autrui devient chez chacun de nous le devoir continu qui résulte rigoureusement de ce fait irrécusable—vivre par autrui" (*Cat.* 266). To a Christian the words have a tenfold force.

determines the form." "Man is not a result of the world, and yet he depends upon it."[1] The observed variations in the constancy of the relations of nature and man are not sufficient to disturb our confidence in the fixity of what we call natural laws. And, conversely, while the laws remain fixed, man is so far capable of modifying the elements through which their action is displayed, as to seriously alter their total effect. If again we regard only living forms, here the power of man is supreme. Some die away at his approach; others follow him; others are capable of receiving what we are forced to call the moral impress of his character.

To pursue in any detail the consequences which flow from this connection of man with the physical world would be impossible here. It must be enough to notice the general lessons which it teaches as to the action of man and the destiny of creation. As to the first, it shows that the sovereignty of man is manifested, not in the direct exertion, but in the guidance of force.[2] The effect in each case depends not so much on power as on wisdom. In other words, our true strength lies in taking each discovered law as the rule according to which we may employ our energies, always remembering that the higher phenomena rest upon and include the lower, and are modifiable in direct proportion to their complexity.

On the other hand, as man is at present continually modifying all nature, both spontaneously and of purpose, it is necessary to regard the connection thus established as in some sense permanent. We cannot wholly sever the fate of the lower and humbler companions of man, for example, from the fate of man himself. And perhaps there is nothing more characteristic of Comte than the almost importunate eagerness with which he claims for the animals,

[1] *Cat.* 42, 37. [2] *Cat.* 105 ff.

which habitually labour with man to secure his worthy objects, incorporation, according to their individual dignity and services, in the great being into which man himself passes.[1]

VII

Now these grand and far-reaching ideas of the continuity, the solidarity, the totality of life, which answer equally to the laws of our being and the deepest aspirations of our souls, are not only reconcilable with Christianity, but they are essentially Christian. The Positivist theory, so far from advancing anything novel in such teaching, simply places us once again in the original Christian point of view of the Cosmos. Once again the divinity of the Gospel is vindicated by its power, when honestly interpreted, to stand abreast or in advance of the noblest generalisations of experience. And this is in virtue of its essential constitution, intellectually no less than spiritually. For, because it is contained primarily in facts, and not in words, it rises beyond the possible associations of a single age to a full harmony with universal life. And so, as our view of life becomes fuller and richer, our view of the Gospel, which is the transfiguration of life, becomes fuller and richer in the same degree. Doctrine which is based upon the Incarnation or the Resurrection must be progressive, organic, and total. These facts, however imperfectly interpreted, yet mark human existence by an advance in a definite direction, by relation to one centre, by approximation towards a perfect ideal. They contain a principle of continuous life, a principle of social unity, a prospect of "the restoration of all things." And this, too, was the case before history

[1] *Cat.* 31.

or science had laid open the general laws of human progress or the necessary connection of man with the world.

Nor, while the facts in themselves are found to be thus pregnant, does the Apostolic interpretation of the facts in any degree fall short of the meaning which has been assigned to them. "It was the purpose of GOD," we read, "that, in the dispensation of the fulness of times, He might sum up all things in Christ, the things in the heavens and the things upon the earth."[1]

Because of Christ's Incarnation and Passion, "GOD also highly exalted Him, and gave unto Him the name which is above every name, that in the name of Jesus every knee should bow, of things in heaven, and things on earth, and things under the earth."[2]

From Christ,—"which is the head,"—"all the body fitly framed and knit together through that which every joint supplieth, according to the working in due measure of each several part, maketh the increase of the body unto the building up of itself in love."[3]

"The earnest expectation of the creation waiteth for the revealing of the sons of GOD . . . groaning and travailing in pain together until now."[4]

Such language, in its assured confidence, passes our hope; and as we ponder on it, we may well doubt whether even to St. Paul himself the infinite depths of wisdom which it contains were open as they are to us now. Here also it seems as if the lapse of ages and the slow widening of thought could alone adequately reveal the significance of prophecy.[5]

But Christianity does not pause where Positivism pauses, in the visible order. It carries the unity of being yet further, and links all that is seen with that unseen which

[1] Eph. i. 10. [2] Phil. ii. 9, 10. [3] Eph. iv. 16.
[4] Rom. viii. 19, 22. [5] Compare 1 Pet. i. 10-12.

can only be figured to us in parables. An imperious instinct asserts that our individual existence is not closed by what falls here under our senses; and every indication of the intimate relationship of man with man, and of age with age, confirms the belief in the further extension of this law of dependence to an order of being beyond the present. If we further take account of the many tokens of a scheme begun and not completed here, which requires for the present the sacrifice of races, it may be, or of generations, the same conviction is deepened. Even in the constitution and advance of society, the effects of selfishness and sin are so open and great, that we are forced to look onward to some future resolution of the discords by which they interrupt the harmony of life.

From the nature of the case, it is impossible that we should have any distinct apprehension of this unseen order. Our utmost resources of language only enable us to combine variously the phenomena with which we are already acquainted; and this to which we are looking is a new order, and not the transference of the old to a new sphere. But though our notions of the future must be vague, Christianity so treats it as to assure us of our personal hope, and at the same time to indicate the direction in which we may look for the solution of the mysteries of society.

In the first place, it accepts unequivocally the indivisibility of man.[1] The body is not a burden by which the soul is temporarily weighed down, but an essential condition of our personality, to be won[2] and disciplined, and in the end to be transfigured, but not destroyed. The central fact in which these truths are conveyed is absolutely unique, as is the combination of the truths themselves. Between the Resurrection and any of the other raisings from the dead there is no more resemblance than there is between

[1] Compare *Cat.* 24. [2] Compare 1 Thess. iv. 4 (κτᾶσθαι).

the Incarnation and any of the fabled visits of the Greek gods to earth in human shapes. The same event which declares the essential permanence of our whole being shows that the conditions of its action and existence will be changed. In what way this change will be accomplished we cannot tell. We know only that we can draw no conclusions from the limitations of this world as to the character of the next, and, on the other hand, that nothing in us will be lost.

Corresponding reflections help us to see how that which appears to be lost or prematurely carried away here may have truly fulfilled its work. It is clear that performance is not a final test of character, nor external action of effect. We are conscious of subtle powers about us, which cannot be analysed or resisted. In another order, as we can believe, we may be allowed to see how these had their origin in silent, unnoticed, or forgotten souls, which will then be revealed in the plenitude of their true energy.

The mystery of evil, we allow, still remains; but even on this light is cast. It ceases, at least, to be triumphant or active.

"Then cometh the end when [Christ] shall deliver up the kingdom to GOD, even the Father; when He shall have abolished all rule, and all authority and power. For He must reign till He hath put all His enemies under His feet. The last enemy that shall be abolished is death. . . . Then shall the Son also Himself be subjected to Him that did subject all things unto Him, that GOD may be all in all."[1]

This sublime prospect lies before us, in which all the varied developments of life are crowned with their divine fulfilment. And though the contemplation of it may lie without the range of the personal teaching of Christianity which commonly limits our religious thought, yet it is a duty to strive, as occasion may arise, to grasp the full pro-

[1] 1 Cor. xv. 24 ff.

portions of the hope which it brings to man and to the world. It is not always enough that each should feel in his own heart the power of the Gospel to meet individual wants. We must claim for it also to be recognised as a wisdom revealed and realised only in the advance of time, and embracing in one infinite fact all that men have aspired to for themselves and for the transitory order in which they are placed.

It is our lot to live in an age when this need is imperative. On all sides there is a restless striving after some solid construction of truth which may rise out of and above the results of negative criticism. Never before were the evils of dispersive study more apparent or more pressing. Never before were isolated views of truth more capable of being exhibited in their one-sidedness. Never before was anarchy of thought and life felt to be more at variance with the highest destiny of man. Never before was there a more passionate longing for spiritual unity among those whom the conditions of life have separated. Of all these facts the teaching of Positivism is an unlooked-for and unsuspected witness. At the same time it seems to point out how we may apply the Apostolic message to combine, and supplement, and guide, and animate the scattered elements out of which the future may be worthily built. And while we thankfully receive the lessons which it gives, we owe to it also a new confirmation of our historic creed. For if anything external can reassure faith, it must be that the widest interpretation of human progress, the subtlest analysis of human nature, is only a partial commentary on the Resurrection.

APPENDIX II

THE RESURRECTION OF CHRIST A NEW REVELATION[1]

I

It is greatly to be regretted that those who enter on the examination of religious questions do not in every case state distinctly the postulates which underlie their reasoning. As it is, serious misunderstanding arises from the use of words which carry with them wholly different associations, according as they are used on one side or the other; and discussions which profess to be impartial are conducted, it may be even unconsciously, in the interest of foregone conclusions. It is obvious, for example, that the idea of a "sign" or "miracle" is, under particular circumstances, natural or unnatural according as a man believes, or does not believe, in a Creator who is still in a living connection with His creation. If, again, it is assumed that a revelation is impossible, the belief in a revelation *must* be a delusion, and the records which give an account of its delivery *must* be incredible. This being so, it is clear that the charge which is habitually urged against so-called "apologists," of being committed to the conclusion which they have to

[1] This essay originally appeared in the *Contemporary Review*, November 1877.

establish, applies more completely to the "alogists," who deny the possibility of revelation altogether. The "apologist" is perfectly free to modify his view of the methods of revelation, to strive to gain a fuller conception of the unity of the Divine plan, to seek for a more comprehensive survey of "nature," as embracing the utmost potency of being which falls within the grasp of his powers; but the "alogist" has barred his own progress by an absolute negation. "This and this," he ventures to say, "cannot be: if it is ever said to have been, the statement is inherently false. All that remains for the critic is to explain as plausibly as he can how the statement gained currency."

I propose, therefore, in the present paper to state as clearly as I can under what conditions the Christian enters on an examination of the evidence for the Resurrection, what is the Evangelic conception of the fact itself, how the fact thus interpreted illustrates the character of the Christian faith generally as a historical faith, how it bears upon our views of the world and upon studies of present interest. It is obviously impossible to do more than indicate lines of thought in these different directions. The examination of the details of evidence belongs to another place. But a general view of the Christian position, apart from other advantages, will show that some of the attacks directed against it are based on misconceptions.

Three final assumptions are made everywhere throughout the Bible. It is assumed (1) that God is, and that He is righteous and loving; (2) that man was made in the image of God; and (3) that man has fallen. It is taken for granted that these statements correspond with man's constitution, and that he is directly conscious of their truth. They lie beyond the region of debate. It is indeed possible to show not only that they fall in with what we can observe, but that the sum of experience illustrates and confirms them; still, if they be denied, argument is useless. No "proof" can establish the existence of a Heavenly Father, the GOD of conscience, and not "the Absolute Being" of ontology. No "proof" can show beyond contradiction that we can hold intercourse with Him, the finite with the Infinite. No "proof" can demonstrate that that which is to lift us up must be outside us and above us. But we claim that these ultimate facts are given in germ, in consciousness. We claim that those who have attained to the maturity of self-knowledge under normal conditions recognise them as true. They form for us the presuppositions of all religious controversy.[1]

Assumptions of the same kind underlie all reasoning; they are not peculiar to theology. The belief in the external world, and the belief in our own personal responsibility, rest on grounds exactly similar to those which support the belief in a Heavenly Father. Each of these three ultimate beliefs is open to specious objections: each belief is maintained by the requirements and the experience of living.

Several important conclusions follow immediately from these assumptions. If GOD is the Father of men, it becomes probable that He will under certain circumstances make His presence felt by peculiar "signs," and that these "signs" will bear a definite relation both to the divine lessons with which they are connected and to the persons to whom the lessons are addressed. It becomes probable, further, that, when the discipline of humanity is regarded on a large scale, these special manifestations of the Divine will appear to be analogous to crises in the development

[1] This is not the place to explain more at length or to defend these presuppositions. I wish simply to mark clearly the position which Christian critics occupy. It is evident that all examination of evidence involves some presuppositions.

of the individual life, in which exceptional powers are active for a time and then subside, all being harmonious parts of one life. And again, to look at the subject from another point of sight, if we derive our being, it matters not through what descent, from a good Creator, each natural desire or instinct of man carries with it the promise of fulfilment. It is not conceivable that he should have been endowed with aspirations which must always remain unsatisfied. He may be unable beforehand to anticipate how they will be satisfied; he may even form false and confident anticipations; but after the event it must be discernible that the satisfaction is real. If we feel that the scheme of things in which we are placed is true, if we feel, that is, that the apparent signs of progress which it exhibits reveal its essential nature, we cannot doubt that the characteristic tendencies of human action and feeling and thought are also true, and turned towards that which we are made to attain to. It cannot, then, be in vain that we instinctively look forward to a nobler future and a closer fellowship with GOD hereafter; and turn heavenward, as knowledge widens, for some fuller teaching as to these loftiest hopes. No doubt our instincts, both physical and moral, require to be disciplined and trained; but they are in a real sense prophetic. While they are not, in our present condition, authoritative, they are suggestive.

Thus revelation, which is only one form of the continuous intercourse of GOD and man, so far from being improbable, is seen from the actual circumstances of life to be a natural consequence of the Divine Fatherhood. It is in regard to the life of the society as natural as prayer in the life of the individual. Prayer in fact presupposes revelation, for it is man's answer to the voice of GOD. And the thoughts of revelation and prayer illustrate one another in other ways. The mode of revelation, for instance, may be expected to vary from age to age, just as the scope of prayer. As man advances in the knowledge of GOD, he will at each point in his progress fashion his thoughts of Him in harmony with the sum of all he knows.

Nor can it be fairly said that such a view of the living relation between GOD and man and the world as is assumed by the Christian introduces any confusion into his view of the order in which he is placed. It simply substitutes the conception of a rational order for the conception of a mechanical order. All action is based upon the supposition that man can himself, within certain limits, modify the medium in which he moves, and the personal influence of each man is absolutely incalculable, yet this indeterminate factor introduces no practical disharmony into the universe; and it is obviously impossible that this special action, which (it is assumed) answers to perfect wisdom, should do so. Alogists habitually discuss miracles as if they were supposed to be arbitrary manifestations of power, and not essentially connected with a moral purpose and adapted to the wants of those to whom they were granted. If they were arbitrary they would have no theological value. The "signs" of GOD would cease to be "signs" unless they illustrated what we can recognise as a divine law of progress.[1]

For nothing external, no "sign," has an absolute or irresistible force. Every alleged "sign" must be carefully interpreted and brought to a spiritual test. As a "sign" of GOD it must be consistent with all that we already know

[1] Such a statement as that of Mr. Macan (for example), "If miracles are possible, history is impossible" (p. 116, note), is only intelligible on an assumption which a Christian utterly denies. I should venture to say that Christianity alone gives a stable foundation to history, as showing the law and end of life. Viewed in relation to the whole history of the Church or of the world, "miracles" take an intelligible place in the development and interpretation of life.

of Him; and the same power which enables us in the first instance to recognise God, enables us also to recognise further manifestations of His nature and will.[1]

The order of the universe which the Christian maintains is therefore as real as that of the alogist, and as truly verifiable, while it is vaster. Both orders correspond with abstractions which are based upon observation; but the Christian order regards the seen as standing in a vital connection with the unseen, and under the necessary limitations of our present human faculties presents potentially the completest synthesis of being which we can conceive. The occurrence of "signs" causes no break in the continuity of history: on the contrary, they indicate something more as to the nature of the whole life which history expresses. Nor again, is any function of historical criticism dependent on the assumption that facts of a particular kind are impossible. The object of criticism is to test the records of a belief, and then comes the interpretation of the belief. The recorded instances of revelation are for the believer so many elements of which he takes due account in his view of the whole system of phenomena which is offered for his devout study. Little by little he is enabled to apprehend the course of things according to its true law, till the distinction of "natural" and "supernatural" is lost in the perception of the one will of God wrought out in many ways and parts throughout the whole range of creation which falls under our notice.

[1] The full significance of these statements will appear, on a careful examination of the following typical passages: Deut. xiii. 1 ff.; Ezek. xiv. 4 ff.; Matt. xxiv. 23 f.; 2 Thess. ii. 8 ff.; Apoc. xiii. 13 f.

II

These general remarks enable us to approach the consideration of the Resurrection from the true point of sight. For the believer the Resurrection is the crowning revelation of God, the sign of the continuity of the fulness of human being through the seen into the unseen. Under this aspect it is not open to objection on the ground that it is "contrary to experience," for its significance is affirmed to consist in the fact that it is absolutely without parallel. It cannot be said to be even improbable, if it can be shown to convey that teaching as to the future of creation which we are constituted to expect. The alogist utterly misunderstands the state of the case when he persistently represents the Resurrection of Christ as one of many raisings from the dead.[1] If it were no more than this, it could not form the foundation of a Gospel. The fact was, as we maintain, essentially unique; the teaching which it conveyed was essentially new.

A twofold difficulty stands in the way of a just estimate of the novelty of the teaching of the Resurrection. It is difficult to realise the absence of a great and familiar idea; it is difficult also to leave room, so to speak, for larger aspects of a fact which we seem to have felt already in all its grandeur. And thus it comes to pass that the revelation given us by Christ's rising is in one direction spoken of as "commonplace," and in another it is unconsciously neglected. Part of the truth signified by it has passed so completely into modern thought that we can hardly imagine that men were ever without the sure trust that death is the personal admission to the nearer Presence of God. Part of it again is only now at last dawning upon

[1] *E.g. Supernatural Religion*, iii. 428 n.

us: and we are in danger of refusing to recognise the new light, though in this respect it is not hard to see how the original Apostolic message meets the latest results of time.

Something at least has been gained by recent discussions. It is admitted on all sides that the first disciples believed that the Lord had been raised from the dead; it is admitted also that the eleven Apostles and St. Paul believed that they had seen Him after the Resurrection. Historical evidence, alone, can go no further than this. It cannot do more than establish the reality of the belief in a particular fact. The belief is itself the interpretation of phenomena which cannot be recalled, and, in every case, only one of several conceivable interpretations. It is obviously impossible to preserve completely the grounds on which the belief was embraced. These may, indeed, be indicated more or less completely, but it is easy to see that details, which find no record, may have been rightly decisive at the moment. Thus our judgment on the truth of a belief is to be decided mainly by the character of the belief and by the circumstances of those who first held it. In the case of the Resurrection the question at issue is simply, in one form or other, Is it more reasonable to suppose that the Apostles were mistaken or that the Lord did rise? Or, to break the question into its parts, What was the character of the belief? And, Can the belief, with its results, be explained from the actual position of those who held it without the acceptance of the corresponding objective fact?

The general character of the Apostolic belief in Christ's Resurrection may be best seen by regarding the Resurrection in connection with other raisings from the dead. Briefly it may be said that all the other raisings from the dead recorded in the Bible are instances of restoration to the conditions of earthly life: the Resurrection of Christ was the revelation of a new life.[1] The distinction is equally unquestionable and significant. There cannot be the least doubt that those whom the Lord is recorded to have called back to life were afterwards subject to the ordinary circumstances of our present existence. It is no less certain that all the notices of the Risen Lord represent Him as changed while still personally the same. The daughter of Jairus, the young man at Nain, and Lazarus, as far as we can see, resumed their former positions; but the connection of the Lord with the disciples after the Resurrection was wholly altered. He was known only when He pleased to reveal Himself. He was surrounded with a mysterious awfulness. At the very time when He offered a material test of the reality of His presence He showed that He was not bound by the laws of matter. There is evidently a "law" by which the conditions of His appearances are determined. And these contrasted traits are preserved in the different narratives with perfect consistency, so that it is impossible to doubt that the disciples believed that the Lord lived again after the Passion, and yet under new and glorious conditions of life hitherto unrealised. For such a conception they had absolutely no precedent. To speak of it as a "ruling idea" of their age is to misrepresent facts. On the contrary, it was to them a most difficult and strange idea. They thought at first that "they saw a spirit," and this impression had to be overcome. So far as they had any acquaintance with a rising again, their notions were directly at variance with the circumstances of the Lord's Resurrection. The language of Herod and of the people who identified the Lord with John the Baptist raised from the dead, or with one of the prophets, so far as it had any serious meaning, indicates no capacity for a belief in a

[1] I do not enter on the discussion of Matt. xxvii. 52 f. The incident recorded there is wholly isolated.

Resurrection such as that by which the Church lived. And as a matter of experience the popular conceptions of a carnal Resurrection very speedily overpowered the teaching of the New Testament in the early Church.[1]

From this point of sight the importance of the two chief "moments" in the history of the Resurrection becomes obvious. The tomb in which the body of the Lord was laid was found empty. The Lord appeared and disappeared at pleasure. All that belonged to His humanity was preserved, and at the same time all was transfigured. This twofold conception, presented with perfect simplicity and perfect distinctness by the Evangelists, was entirely unparalleled; and *it* includes teaching which has not yet been popularly appropriated.

This being so, it will be seen that no misunderstanding of the Christian idea of the Resurrection can be more complete than that which is involved in the following dilemma:—

> One or other alternative must be adopted:—If Jesus possessed his own body after his resurrection and could eat and be handled, he could not vanish; if he vanished, he could not have been thus corporeal.[2]

The very point of the revelation lies in the reconciliation of these two aspects of the Lord's humanity. The one assures us in the only way in which, as far as we can see, the assurance could be given, that nothing is lost in the passage through death; the other that the limitations which belong to earthly existence are not to be extended to the future order.

The full power of this complex conception is gathered

[1] Any one who will take the trouble to verify in detail the facts indicated summarily in this paragraph, will learn a valuable lesson on the historical characteristics of the Gospels.

[2] *S. R.* iii. 462.

up in the fact of the Ascension, which is the natural or necessary sequel of the Resurrection according to the Christian view. The manifestations of the Risen Christ, as recorded in the Gospels, lead up to it. The history of the forty days shows a gradual preparation of the disciples for the realisation of a spiritual presence of Christ with His Church. So long He allowed them to feel that He was moving locally among them. Then He made it clear by a sensible sign that He had entered on a new state. Thus, the Resurrection rightly interpreted includes the Ascension; and conversely, the Ascension finally interprets the Resurrection for men and under the forms of common thought. That visible lifting from the earth marked the close of one epoch of revelation and the beginning of another. Henceforward the Lord was recognised as throned in glory on the right hand of GOD, near alike to all His people.

But it will be said that the view which has been given of the Resurrection is an "inference" from the records. The statement is true; and true necessarily. It is only by inference, by interpretation, that we can obtain an adequate conception of a fact which belongs to two orders. The Risen Christ belongs to earth and to heaven. If His Resurrection and His raised manhood were of earth only, it might be possible, perhaps, to imagine how any single observer might have ascertained the fact by outward observation, though it is clear that he could not have transmitted his assurance to others. But as it is, no external tests could have established what is of the essence of the fact, the permanence of the old under new conditions not expressed by the "laws" of this world. On the contrary, if external tests alone were satisfied, the very ground of our hope would be destroyed. That which is the strength of the Christian now would be taken away.

In this respect the Christian view of the Resurrection,

as an interpretation of all the phenomena recorded, corresponds with the interpretation of every other divine sign. No external phenomenon in itself can prove the existence of an Almighty GOD. But if we believe that GOD is, then we can learn, through the world without, lessons as to His character and will. There will, however, always remain a way of evasion for the unbeliever. Even if he admits the accuracy of the original observation, and the completeness of the testimony to the observed facts, it will still be possible to refer whatever is exceptional in them to some unknown force simply sufficient to produce the given effect. In other words, the presuppositions of belief underlie the interpretations of belief.

It is therefore quite true in one sense that the Resurrection "proves" nothing. It has no constraining power to compel assent to any proposition; but it is the crowning "sign" of the counsel of GOD for men. It comes to satisfy aspirations, to illuminate doubts, to confirm and define faith. That which St. John observes of the effect of "the beginning of signs" is fulfilled in this latest sign: *Jesus manifested His glory, and His disciples believed on Him.*

John ii. 11.

This consideration places the narratives of the Gospels in their proper light. They are addressed to those who believe the fact, and are not directly designed to create the belief. They are in this respect, as in all others, a record of a revelation. When this is once recognised, it will be seen how completely most of the criticism of the parallel narratives of the Resurrection falls to the ground. There is not the least reason to suppose that the Evangelists told us all that they knew, nor yet the least necessity that they should have done so. They recorded what was sufficient for their purpose. And there can be no doubt that the Gospels both severally and collectively bring before us the Risen Lord as the same and yet changed; as having entered with His perfect Manhood on a new form of existence; as having established in His glorified humanity a new connection with mankind; as having led His disciples by His personal intercourse to grasp these novel conceptions as their abiding heritage.

Now whether this revelation be accepted or not, it cannot be doubted that it was original and pregnant with consequences. But it has been frequently said that the Apostles lived in "an atmosphere of miracles"; that they could not but have framed some explanation to remove the disappointment caused by their Master's death; and that "it was inevitable that they should believe Him to have risen again in the body."[1] It might be sufficient to reply that there is, as we have already seen, no parallel to the Resurrection either in its character or in its effects, and that just so far as the idea could be shown to be familiar it would be deprived of its efficacy. If the belief was "inevitable" it would also have been powerless to change opinion and life. But, as far as evidence exists, the claim to work miracles was not common in the first age, unless the practice of exorcism be brought under this head. On the contrary, it is most remarkable that the miracles of Jewish history belong to critical periods of comparatively short duration, and to typical men. The age of the Maccabees is not marked by miracles. "*John wrought no miracle.*" It is of course quite true that the Jews were acquainted with records of miracles in their Scriptures; quite true also that they could not feel all that is involved in a miracle as we do; but it appears from the Gospels that the works of Christ, though they were often veiled, created a profound impression as being wholly unprecedented. It is at any rate unquestionable that they overcame inveterate prejudices. All this tends to show

John x. 41.

[1] *Contemporary Review*, November 1876, p. 905.

that we are unconsciously tempted to transfer to the whole period of Jewish history phenomena which belong to limited manifestations within it, and to use what sprang from Christianity to explain the origin of Christianity.

A similar remark applies to the alleged prevalence and power of Messianic expectations in the first century. There were indeed some Jews who were looking for the promised King when Christ came, or, perhaps more strictly speaking, *for the Kingdom of God*, or for the *consolation of Israel*. John the Baptist gave distinctness to expectation. But the teaching of John and the earlier teaching of the Lord excited questionings rather than satisfied them. It was only when the Lord's work was drawing to a close that He accepted the title of the Christ from Jews, and then under circumstances which showed how far the confession was not only from popular feeling, but even from the feeling of the disciples. After the appearance of the Lord had called out the religious aspirations of the nation, false Christs arose; but the hopes which they embodied were rather due to Christ's action than originally contributory to His acceptance. He created the idea which He fulfilled in spite of current opinions, and in doing this He gave occasion to the characteristic embodiment of the ideas which He set aside. So far from "answering the ideal" of His followers, He gave them a new one, which they were painfully slow to grasp. Men could not "see" the Kingdom of God which He proclaimed unless they were born again. There was practically nothing in the current thoughts which Christ encountered which was fitted to call out a spontaneous belief in the message of His Resurrection. The silence of the Old Testament, the "bold guesses" and sad negations of Gentile philosophy, are equally instructive. The one shows how Divine wisdom was constrained to delay the revelation till it could be presented vitally: the

Luke ii. 25, 38.

John iii. 3.

other that reason, while baffled by the problem of the future, finds no rest in scepticism. When Christ came this only remained to men as the issue of ages of resolute and patient thought, that the instinct by which they clung to a continuous personality beyond the grave was at hopeless variance with such an analysis of their own being as they could make.

To reconcile this antagonism there was need of a new fact. And this fact was given, as we have seen, in a manner suited to the end. For that end it was enough to show in a single example the fulness of life undiminished by death; to show that what seems to be dissolution is transformation; that heaven lies about us, and that life eternal is not future but present; that whatever be the unknown glories and endowments of the after-life, nothing is cast off which rightly claims our affection and reverence in this.

But it may yet be said that the Evangelists at any rate write as if they were dealing with ordinary phenomena, that they show no perception of the marvellous or contradictory character of the incidents which they relate. The Evangelists certainly write as members of a society in which the divine action was felt to be a present reality manifested in many ways. If they had recorded miracles calmly, and lived ordinary lives, there might be some force in the objection; but it is undeniable that their action corresponded with their words. If they wrote as men to whom the "supernatural" was familiar, they lived so too. Everything which the first Christians did, as well as everything which they said, so far as we know, showed a supreme conviction that they were living in an unexampled crisis. Heaven (so they said, and their work answered to their words) was open about them, and the effects of their teaching corresponded with the conviction.

For the belief in the Resurrection was from the first not a belief only, but a spring of energy. The disciples were not only assured that their Lord was living: they felt that He was with them, and their conduct answered to the reality of the feeling. It is not then sufficient to show how a belief in the rising of Christ might have been created among men familiar with the idea of the Resurrection as we are. The problem to be solved is how a belief was created which, from the first even till now, has made believers act as knowing that it is literally true that when two or three are gathered together in Christ's name, there He is in the midst of them. This we may safely assert was a "new idea introduced into human consciousness," and fruitful beyond all example.[1] Later visions, so far from explaining its origin, serve only as faint reflections to witness to its power.

The Resurrection, to set the matter in another light, was not an isolated event. It was and is an abiding fact. It was the beginning of a new and living relation between the Lord and His people. He came to them while He went. The idea may be expressed by saying that the Apostolic conception of the Resurrection is rather "the Lord lives," than "the Lord was raised." This important truth is entirely overlooked by critics who lay stress on the point that "there was no eye-witness of the Resurrection."[2] It is impossible to see what we should have gained by the testimony of such a witness, or what he could have established which was not established by the intercourse of the living Lord with His disciples. That which had to be made clear as to Christ, was the reality of His new life. This was first established for the Apostles by their complete

[1] Mr. Macan fails to apprehend the idea of the Resurrection when he denies this, p. 108.

[2] *S. R.* pp. 449, 549; Macan, p. 28.

experience of the continuity of His manifestation to them, and for the Church in all ages through the signs of His power. And it is here that the "proof" of the Resurrection is to be found. Christ lives, for He works still.

I have spoken of the Resurrection as a revelation; it was a revelation in two main respects—as to the relation of Christ to men, and as to the relation of the present life to the future. In both these respects it is undeniable that the belief in the Resurrection completely changed the views of the disciples. Before the Passion they had been unable to endure the thought of any external separation from Christ; afterwards they lived in effectual fellowship with Him though He was invisible. His influence was felt to be confined within no local limits. An entirely new connection was shown in life to be established between One and all, between the Son of Man and men. The disciples looked for His return, but the mode in which they conceived of His being preserved them, though in many cases not their followers, from sensuous imaginings of its nature.

For the Apostles' view of the life of the Risen Christ was in close dependence on their view of the relation of believers to Him. His being was continuous with that which they had known; but it was become infinitely glorious, without being deprived of anything belonging to the perfection of humanity.

These two thoughts together opened a prospect of the future of individuals which is far larger than the popular conceptions of later times. Believers were to be transfigured and at the same time their life was to continue in Christ. In other words, a glimpse was given of a "personality" of a raised humanity, in which each member was included but not absorbed.

At the same time light was thrown upon the dark mysteries of sin and suffering. The uttermost sorrow was the preparation for the most complete triumph. Once for all, that dualism to which the phenomena of this world taken by themselves seem to point was shown to be false.

Nor can we stop at man. The Apostles felt that the Resurrection had a message in regard to all creation. Man was bound up with the whole visible order, and this, too, was, as they announced, to partake of his restoration, and to be included in the divine consummation of all things.

Such a final unity, to touch upon the last mystery of all, is referred to an archetypal unity. The Resurrection appears, in the New Testament, as the fulfilment through victory of a purpose involved in creation, but checked in its normal progress by the self-assertion of the finite.[1]

Now such thoughts as these evidently reach to the last problems of life, and illuminate them. Such thoughts flow directly from the Resurrection if the fact be accepted simply as it is presented to us in the Gospels; and, as it is admitted, they were set forth by the Apostles in virtue of their belief in it. Our contention is that nothing but the fact can explain their origin, and the power with which they were propagated. The reality of the Resurrection and the action of the Spirit of the Risen Christ is a sufficient cause for the announcement and for the spread of the Gospel, and no other has been brought forward.

But when stress is laid upon the correspondence of the Gospel of the Resurrection with man's nature, it is said that that very correspondence furnishes a presumption that man devised that which answered to his wishes. There is, however, a wide difference between recognising and creating. All pre-Christian experience is unfavourable to the theory that man had any tendency to find such a solution of his difficulties as the Resurrection offers. The whole discipline

[1] This truth is plainly expressed in Col. i. 15 ff., and does not remain to be "excogitated," Macan, p. 141.

of the world prepared men to welcome the Gospel, but had no power to produce it. And this second correspondence of the Resurrection with the course of human progress, no less than with the constitution of man, forms another strong sign of its divine reality to every one who believes in a Providence. To such a one, it is not too much to say that the Resurrection, taken in connection with the history of the race before and after, is antecedently more probable than any particular event in the life of any individual man. So far is it from being contrary to "universal experience," that it is in a most true sense according to universal experience, for it is seen universally that aspirations, tendencies, instincts, are not left for ever unattained and unsatisfied.[1]

If now we consider the direct evidence for the fact of the Resurrection from this position, it will be found to be overwhelming. It is, of course, idle to affect to discuss evidence for an event if it is laid down that the event "is at once disposed of on abstract grounds,"[2] or to insist on the testimony of documents which record miracles if "a supernatural phenomenon is to be at once rejected"; for on this assumption they are already declared to be untrustworthy. But if the Resurrection and the testimony by which it is maintained are examined in the light of a belief in the Providential government of the world, of a belief, that is, that there is a purpose and a goal for man, and men, and nature, then it is difficult to see how the evidence could have been, according to the analogy of history, more complete. We have, in the Synoptic Gospels and the appendix to St. Mark (to summarise results which appear

[1] But for a strange misunderstanding of this sentence I should have thought it unnecessary to say that the Resurrection of Christ does seem to me to give the satisfaction which we need now in our present life, which is, as I have endeavoured to show, completely transfigured by it in every region of thought and observation and work.

[2] *S. R.* iii. 522.

to me to be unquestionable), a general view of the oral teaching of the Twelve, which was the original foundation of the Church: we have in the writings of St. Paul, who must have been well acquainted with the earliest belief of Christians, an explicit statement of what he "received" and taught with intense personal conviction won through experience: we have in the Gospel of St. John the personal testimony of one who had actually seen and heard the Risen Lord; and these three distinct lines of evidence are in complete accordance as to the reality, the nature, and the effects of the Resurrection of Christ. It is utterly unhistorical to say that

> the whole of the evidence for the Resurrection reduces itself to an undefined belief on the part of a few persons, in a notoriously superstitious age, that after Jesus had died and been buried they had seen him alive.[1]

The belief of the original witnesses was so clear that it completely revolutionised their national expectations; so energetic that it changed their whole character; so vivid that it was from the very first expressed in rites which symbolise with most remarkable power the fundamental thought of life through death. It answers questions which men cannot but ask, and that in a way wholly unanticipated and coextensive with the utmost range of knowledge; it is supported, not only by specific testimony, which, from the nature of things, must be partial and fragmentary and capable of misinterpretation, but by that underlying trust in the reality of the divine government and the divine destiny of creation which is "practically infinite." For the direct voice of testimony is a very small part of the evidence by which the Resurrection is established. The Resurrection explains, as nothing else can explain, the acts and words of Christ before it, and of His Apostles after it; it gives a

[1] *S. R.* p. 519.

sufficient reason for the spiritual power and insight of the first Christians, which is different in kind from all that went before; it explains the life of Christendom, for it is not a past event only, but a fact attested by its present efficacy, by the signs of an actual union of believers with the Son of Man operative in life. If, now, we give fair weight to all these considerations, upon the assumptions which have been laid down,—to the personal attestation of the fact by the Apostles, to the circumstances under which St. Paul was led to proclaim it, to its relation to Christ's whole work, to the transformation which it effected in the opinions and conduct of the first disciples, to its continuous efficiency in life, to its consilience with instinct, to its harmony with what we can see of the divine discipline of the world,—I find no reason to modify what I have said elsewhere, that, "taking all the evidence together, there is no single historical incident better or more variously supported than the Resurrection of Christ."

Let any one who thinks otherwise endeavour to frame for himself evidence for the whole fact—for the fact, that is, as belonging to two orders, the seen and the unseen, and uniting them—which he thinks would have been more satisfactory than that which we possess, and then candidly determine how far the modifications which he has introduced would have removed his difficulties, and how far they would have detracted from the significance of the fact as a "sign," a Divine Revelation.

III

The view which has been given of the Resurrection as a Revelation will serve to show in what sense Christianity is said to be "a historical religion." The phrase is ambiguous, and, as applied to Christianity, it is persistently misinterpreted by critics who speak of Buddhism or Mohammedanism as "historical" in the same sense. It is true, no doubt, that these three religions are so far alike that they owe their origin to historical personages. It is possible to fix their beginning and progress with more or less completeness in connection with definite circumstances. But it is not in this relation that Christianity is described as historical. Christianity is described as a historical religion because its teaching—in regard to its doctrines, its motives, its promises —is conveyed in facts.

In this respect the Gospel is absolutely unique. The Lord claimed to come, not as a prophet, but as One greater than prophet or temple, as "the Truth and the Life." And as such He was preached and accepted. What the Apostles proclaimed was a Person who had died and risen again, by whose Death and Resurrection light, as they affirmed, was thrown upon the final mysteries of being. They very rarely quote His words, but everywhere speak of what He was and is, of His work, of His power, of His presence.

It is impossible to exaggerate the importance of this unquestionable character of the Apostolic message. Nothing can be more certain than that the Apostles did not regard their Lord as one simply who had declared new truths or who had made old truths plainer. Every interpretation of the rise of Christianity must be fatally misleading which does not take Christ's Person, what He did, what befell Him, what He was therefore held to be, as the novel power by which men were moved.

This historical foundation of Christianity is seen most strikingly in the writings of St. Paul. Perhaps we might have expected from his intellectual constitution, and from the circumstances of his conversion, that he would have rested on abstract dogmas, on "the Christ within"; but, in fact, Christ "of the seed of David," "born of a woman, born under the Law," is the centre of his faith. It has been said that it is "a most striking and extraordinary fact that the "life and teaching of Jesus have scarcely a place in the system of Paul."[1] If St. Paul had regarded Christ as a prophet only, the remark would have been just: as it is, so far as it is true, it places in more conspicuous prominence the meaning which St. Paul found in "the blood of Christ," in the historic person and human work of Him "who died and rose again." The facts of Christ's life, the facts which are recited in the earliest creeds, are the revelation of sin and righteousness which he unfolds; they are never absent from his mind: without them his teaching is unintelligible.

This truth may be exhibited in another way. In the Epistles of St. Paul, no less than in the preaching recorded in the Acts, the facts of the Faith precede the dogmas And the relation holds good always. The dogmas are the progressive and approximate interpretation of the facts. As the facts are more completely understood the dogmas become more and more fully defined. For this reason the apprehension of Christian truth can never be final, and it can never be exhausted. Each fresh acquisition of knowledge as to the relation of man to man and of man to the world throws light upon Christian work. Teaching necessarily reflects in some measure the modes of thought of the age to which it belongs, but the broad facts of a human life grow more luminous as life itself is more deeply studied. The Death and the Resurrection of the Son of Man are felt by us to mean far more than could have been grasped by an earlier generation.

It is undoubtedly true that at present we receive the facts and the dogmatic interpretation of the facts simultaneously; too often perhaps we are tempted to lose the

[1] *S. R.* iii. 567.

facts in the dogmas. But this circumstance cannot alter the essential relation in which they stand to one another. At every crisis of thought it is our duty to turn again to the records of Christ's work, not in a spirit of superficial realism, but with a strenuous endeavour to follow out, as far as our powers will allow us,[1] the consequences which are involved in that union of the divine and human, of the seen and the unseen, which we believe to have been fulfilled in the present order of life and to remain as the foundation and the goal of hope and faith and love.

This principle, which has an obvious application to our main subject, requires to be insisted upon, because it is frequently overlooked or misunderstood. The Christian Faith, as a system, is the interpretation of the facts of Christ's life in the light of the assumptions which, as we have seen, are everywhere made in the Bible. The interpretation may come in different ways. At one time it is through the inward voice of God, at another time through a better understanding of Apostolic words, at another through the experience of life, at another through the investigation of the "laws" of nature; but in every case the Person of Christ and the facts of His life are the final sum of the eternal Gospel, the abiding test by which every approximation to the fulness of truth is tried.

IV

It follows from what has been said that the belief in Christ's Resurrection is not merely the belief in a past

[1] The unhappy boldness of later speculation on the state of the disembodied spirit, when compared with the silence of Scripture upon the subject, offers an instructive illustration of the neglect of this limitation. It is strange that this contrast should be misunderstood (Macan, pp. 154 ff.).

event, but in a present, or rather in an eternal, fact. It is sometimes said that Romanists are more consistent or more logical than "Anglicans and Protestants," in that they affirm the reality of a present revelation to which the latter make no pretence. The statement is, I venture to believe, a complete misconception. All Christians alike, as I suppose, believe equally in the unbroken intercourse between God and man, which is the essence of revelation; but the Romanist holds to the permanence of old forms in the mode of revelation, while others consider that the mode of revelation, as being a function of life, will vary with the progress of humanity. In one age, or at one period of popular growth, isolated "signs" can be seen to be the most appropriate vehicle for conveying a divine message. In another age or at another period, corresponding lessons may come through the investigation of history or of nature which was impossible before. In each case God speaks to men as they can hear Him, and according to the knowledge which they have gained of Him.

It is most untrue, therefore, to affirm that the frank acceptance of "critical" methods in the investigation of the records of past revelation involves any abandonment of the "supernatural." The study of the Bible in such a spirit enables us undoubtedly to realise a completer harmony between the ordinary processes of thought and action and those which God has been pleased to use for the conveyance of His lessons, but none the less the facts, and the record and interpretation of the facts, retain their divine character wholly unimpaired. The question as to the record (for example) is whether we suppose that the guidance was given directly, or through character, experience, circumstances. In the latter case there is as much room for divine action as in the former; and if it appears that we can most rightly apprehend "inspiration" in the past in this way, we are at once encouraged to look for some manifestations of the Divine will now, which will come also to us through the ordinary channels of life and thought. So far from "criticism" obscuring the work of GOD, it opens our eyes to see it going on about us.

This is not the occasion to pursue such reflections in detail; but certainly nothing is more remarkable than the way in which the Apostolic writers bring out the eternal aspects of the facts which they proclaim, without admixture of anything which was local and temporal. They exhibit in different directions that universality of character which every historian must recognise in Christ. And it is important to notice that this characteristic is derived naturally from the message of the Resurrection which they announced. They felt and they expressed, what we have not yet come to understand, that the belief in the Resurrection "in Christ" carries with it a belief in the continuity, the solidarity, the totality (if I may so speak) of creation. The unity of being, of which science is slowly shaping a conception, was for them a unity of life tending to an issue of unimaginable glory.

The Resurrection, indeed, gives a permanent value to all human effort and achievement. As long as the earth was held to be the everlasting scene of man's dominion, each worker could look forward to an endless life in posterity; but we know now that the earth itself can exist only for a time, and a hope of immortality requires the assurance of life continued under new conditions. This, as we have seen, is exactly what the Apostolic records are fitted to convey. They meet, unexpectedly as it might appear, a difficulty of the latest time; they receive illustration from researches supposed to be alien in scope and spirit.

In this respect, as in all points, the Gospel of the Resurrection answers to the whole sum of life. The fact of the

Resurrection is as divinely original as the character of Christ. It adds the element of continuance, the possibility of consecration, to every earthly interest. It offers the fulness of truth, as against the one-sided materialism which will acknowledge nothing as real but the objects of sense, and the one-sided spiritualism which disparages the outward. It represents, like life itself, a combination of antitheses. But this superficial conflict of elements is inevitable as long as man is regarded in action. For the present we must speak, even as we must think, according to the limitations which are imposed upon us. But these limitations are shown, in Christ, not to be inherent in our personality. Our individual personality is shown to be contributory to some vaster "personality." The unity of which we are conscious becomes the figure of a unity of humanity, of a unity of creation.

THE END

Printed by R. & R. Clark, Limited, *Edinburgh.*